The Book of Ancient Wisdom

R RADHAKRISHNAN

Published by Radhakrishnan R, 2022.

While every precaution has been taken in the preparation of this book, the publisher assumes no responsibility for errors or omissions, or for damages resulting from the use of the information contained herein.

THE BOOK OF ANCIENT WISDOM

First edition. October 20, 2022.

Copyright © 2022 R RADHAKRISHNAN.

ISBN: 979-8215422502

Written by R RADHAKRISHNAN.

Also by R RADHAKRISHNAN

The Temples of India
The Temples of India: Somnathapura, Mysore

Travellers Tales
Rustic Romeo

Standalone
The Colors of Life
The Temples of India : Guruvayur
Indian Mythology
The Book of Ancient Wisdom

Watch for more at https://sites.google.com/view/rradhakrishnan.

Table of Contents

*My mother Saraswathi and my grandmothers for all the
stories that I grew up with.*

Foreword

India is an ancient land and Indian civilisation is the oldest surviving civilisation as of today.

In India, many faiths originated, cultures grew and civilisations mingled and enriched each other.

Civilisations developed, grew and but never faded out completely as others came up. The new cultures and civilisations just added and built up on the previous one.

This saw an intermingling of ideas, concepts, practices, and beliefs.

Indian civilisation and culture are simple and yet complex. It seems chaotic, unorganised, and makes no sense to the outsider. There seem too many contradictions, too many divergences in the entire process.

But to an Indian, everything seems simple and straightforward. The perceptions of western thought imagines everything in black and white. Indians think in multihued colours, a rainbow, each colour is different but makes an enchanting singularity.

The stories of India are also reflected this.

A story could have different versions, different perspectives depending on the local culture and traditions.

This makes reading Indian tales fun and enlightening.

Each tale may look simple but will have underlying concepts and lessons for living.

Many stories were told orally, and changed with each retelling.

Some of them are stories I read, some are stories I saw, and some stories heard during my travels around the country.

The epics have different written versions. There are oral traditions too, songs, local legends celebrated in local festivals like the Koothandavar festival in Tamil Nadu.

There are also folktales which seem simple but have a universal and relevant lessons even today.

These stories have lessons for life if we choose to accept it. If we do not, then also these are magical tales that enchant and entertain.

I enjoyed retelling these timeless tales; I wish and hope you enjoy reading them.

R. Radhakrishnan

COCHIN, August 2022

Introduction

The Rishis, the wise men of ancient India, were in a dilemma. They had compiled the Vedas, the rules of behaviour, and conceptualised Dharma.

Dharma, you could consider as a mission statement for life.

How can people understand it?

How could they ensure people listened to the lessons?

The wise men came up with the brilliant idea of telling stories which would interest people and contain the required knowledge to learn from.

So were born the marvellous stories and epics of India. The stories teach ideals, morals, rules of life and more, brilliantly packaged in stories that enchant and teach.

The great epics of India, the Ramayana and the Mahabharata, are called ithihasa, which means "this is how it happened".

Many Hindus consider these as history and not stories or mythology.

The Epics, especially the Mahabharata, tell us not only stories, they describe the geography of the land, how people lived, it discusses dharma and rules of living; it tells you the history of its characters and how life was then.

One of the greatest books written in the world, the Gita, is part of the Mahabharata.

These stories have advice on administration, ruling a country, and rules for individual living, which are relevant even today as well.

Travelling storytellers came to a village or a city, people sat around a campfire, and listened as these storytellers captivated them with these tales.

Later, in folk forms like Yakshagana, Kathakali, traditional plays, these stories became dramas, and the storytellers became singers, actors and enacted the stories under flickering lamps.

The next season was yet to start, and the fields were open. These fields became the stage for these plays.

Travelling troupes would enact these stories. Dance drama forms Kathakali or Bharata Natyam were enacted inside the temple premises.

A platform lower than the stages you see now was the stage. The light would be from oil lamps.

No backdrops or any special effects were used.

The musicians and singers would be at the side of the stage. You sat cross-legged on the soft sand of the temple. When you sat like this, the stage height was ideal.

The performance would start after dinner.

Throughout the day, the drummer would drum up a rhythm called the Keli kottu, announcing the play that they would stage that night.

The performance continued all night. We would sit mesmerised as the singer sang the story and the dancers, in traditional colourful Kathakali costumes, brought the story to life with their dance.

It was the old story teller sitting and telling stories around a campfire, but now his stories came to life as actors emoted it.

Now you have performances that are on a modern stage, back drops, sound systems, plush seating, air conditioning and all modern conveniences. The characters came on stage in with oil lamps providing light. This had a charm of its own.

India has many stories in one form or another. There are regional variations and there are folk traditions. There would be minor or major changes. But they all have one thing in common: they enchant and they educate.

The Ramayana a quick glimpse

The Ramayana is the other great epic of India and talks about a period much before the Mahabharata.

The Mahabharata is about a family feud, a falling out among brothers. In earlier days, people avoided keeping the Mahabharata at home. There was a superstition that it would lead to fights within the family.

The Ramayana is a much gentler story, a love story in fact.

Dashrath is the mighty king of Ayodhya who has three wives, Kaushalya, Kaikeyi, and Sumitra.

They have no children and after long prayers and yagnas are blessed with four sons.

Rama, or Sriram, the eldest, was born to Kaushalya. Bharata, younger than Rama, was born to Kaikeyi. Sumitra, the third wife, had two younger sons, Lakshmana and Shatrughna.

Dasharatha is attached to his sons, but Rama is his favourite. Rama is an upright, handsome prince, a great warrior, learned, considerate and sweet-tempered. He is everyone's favourite. All the three queens dote on him, the people love him.

Lakshmana is attached to Rama and Shatrughna to Bharat. But all the three younger brothers are devoted to Rama.

Rama lifts and breaks the giant bow of Shiva and thus wins the hand of Sita, daughter of king Janaka of Mithila.

Rama is an avatar of Vishnu and Sita an avatar of Lakshmi.

Rama marries Sita, and they come back to Ayodhya. A delighted Dasharatha announces Rama will be the crown prince.

Queen Kaikeyi has a servant who has accompanied her from her father's house. Manthra, a hunchbacked crone who fills Kaikeyi's ears and convinces her to get the King declare Bharata as the crown prince. Kaikeyi has brain fade and agrees.

Kaikeyi is the youngest queen, beautiful and the king's favourite. Long ago she had accompanied the King to battle and saved his life. The King grants her two boons which are now invoked by Kaikeyi.

The first boon is that Bharata be made the crown prince. The second is that Rama be banished to the forest for fourteen years. The banishment is because Kaikeyi fears that is Rama remains in the kingdom the people will not accept Bharata as the king.

Dasharatha protests but to no avail. The queen does not relent and he cannot break his promise to her. Rama hears of his father's dilemma from Kaikeyi and cheerfully agrees to the conditions.

Sita and Lakshmana are adamant that they will also accompany him, and they do so.

Dasharatha pines for his beloved son and dies from heartbreak at the separation.

While all this is happening, Bharat and Shatrughna are away from the kingdom.

They return to find the kingdom sunk in mourning at the death of their king and the banishment of their beloved prince Rama.

In the Mahabharata, brothers and family fight for power. The Ramayana is from a more gentle and righteous time.

Bharata is aghast and angry at what his mother has done. He disowns her and refuses the kingdom. He goes with the ministers and the citizens of Ayodhya to bring back Ram and crown him the king.

He meets Ram, Sita and Lakshman and pleads with Rama to come back and rule. But Rama refuses as he says he is duty bound to fulfil his father's promise.

Bharata refuses to rule and finally agrees to rule as a regent for fourteen years till Rama comes back. He takes Rama's footwear and places it on the throne and rules as a regent. During the fourteen years Rama is in the forest, Bharat also lives as an ascetic, forgoing all comforts of the palace. He takes a promise from Rama that he will be back after fourteen years. Bharat vows that if Rama does not come back, Bharata would kill himself by entering the fire.

Rama, Sita and Lakshmana lead a happy life in the forest, having many adventures, meeting holy men and traveling the length and breadth of the land.

Shurpanakha is the sister of Ravana, the mighty king of Lanka. She wants to marry Rama or Lakshmana. When they refuse, she tries to attack Sita. Lakshmana drives her off after cutting her nose.

Shurpanakha complains to her brother and advises him to abduct Sita in revenge, which Ravana does.

Ravana is enamoured with Sita's beauty and wants to marry her.

He cannot do that without her consent or force himself on her because of a curse and keeps her imprisoned in the Ashoka Vatika surrounded by fearsome rakshashis. They keep trying to pressure Sita into accepting Ravana.

Rama searches for Sita and the vanaras, dwellers of the forest help him. Hanuman the vanara becomes close to Rama and is devoted to him. In Rama, Hanuman sees the lord. Hanuman himself is the son of the wind god.

They come to know that Sita is held captive by Ravana and Rama marches to Lanka with the Vanara army.

They cross the sea at Dhanushkodi with the help of a bridge made of rocks. The remains of this bridge are still seen today and called the Rama Setu.

There is a bloody battle and finally Ravana is killed and Sita rescued.

Rama flies home in the Pushpaka Vimana of Ravana and reaches Ayodhya just before Bharata is about to enter the fire.

The family is united and Rama rules Ayodhya, surrounded by his family.

This is just a gist of the original written by Valmiki, the first poet or adhikavi. The Ramayana is a sublime work in verse which teaches us something new every time we read it.

There are many other main versions based on the above. Two of the popular ones written by Tulsidas in the North and Kamban in the south of India.

The Mahabharata a quick glimpse

This book contains some little-known stories from the Mahabharata. This is a small gist of this great epic which is the biggest epic in the world. It will help you understand the context of some stories in this book.

It is said what is not there in the Mahabharata is not there in any other book.

The Mahabharata is one of the two great epics of India. Almost everyone in India knows the gist of the story. This great epic has touched every corner of our country, India.

The original is the Mahabharata by the sage Vyasa, who himself plays a significant part in the story.

Other than the above, there are many other versions. In many parts of India, there are local traditions and stories which are at variance with what is there in the key version.

These local stories add to the charm of this universal tale of two feuding families.

The kingdom of the Kurus is a vast empire which had many illustrious kings. The story narrates the events that led to the great war at Kurukshetra.

There is Bhishma, the crown prince, who takes a vow of celibacy and gives up the throne so that his father, King Shantanu, can marry Satyavati.

Bhishma is the ideal man to rule the kingdom, well trained in the arts of war, Dharma and administration of a kingdom and yet he gives up his responsibility to the country and its people to fulfil his father's desire and lust.

Dhritarashtra and Pandu are brothers, the sons of Bhishma's step brothers, grandsons of Queen Mother Satyavati.

Dhritarashtra is the eldest, but blind, and thus Pandu is crowned the king, which is always a sore point with Dhritarashtra.

Pandu gets cursed that if he enters conjugal relations, has sex, he will die and so he goes to the forest with his two wives, Kunti the elder wife and Madri his second wife.

They crowned Dhritarashtra king, or rather regent, till a proper heir was born, either to him or Pandu.

Dhritarashtra and his wife beget a hundred sons and one daughter. Duryodhana is their eldest child and Dushasana is the second son. These 100 sons were the Kauravas.

Meanwhile, in the forest, with the help of a mantra, Kunti has three sons, Yudhishthira the eldest who is Dharma incarnate, Bhima the strong, and Arjuna the Archer. Madri also has two sons with this mantra, the twins Nakul and Sahadeva. The five sons are called Pandavas, after their father, Pandu.

Because of the curse he has received, Pandu dies when he tries to have sex with Madri. Pandu is cremated in the forest and Madri joins him in the funeral pyre out of guilt.

Kunti comes back to the capital Hastinapur with the five children, who are accepted as the sons of Pandu and brought up as princes befitting their status. The great Guru Dronacharya trains them in the arts of war, ethics, Dharma and about ruling an empire along with their cousins, the Kauravas.

Yudhishtra is the eldest of both the Pandavas and the Kauravas. He is also the best suited for ruling because of his calm nature and adherence to Dharma.

They crown Yudhishtra the Crown Prince, much to the dismay of Duryodhana and Dhritarashtra.

Duryodhana then plots to kill the Pandavas, along with his scheming uncle Shakuni.

In this story of a family struggle for power, step in many characters.

Karna is the abandoned illegitimate child of Kunti born before her marriage.

By the rules of the day, he is also a son of Pandu. He is elder to both Yudhishtra and Duryodhana and has all the qualities to be a great king. A chariot driver and his wife bring up Karna, so they consider Karna a low born person.

No one knows he is the son of Kunti, abandoned when he was born. Karna does not know who his actual parents are. He is much better than all the others as a warrior, but they do not give him his due and taunt him for being a low born.

Only Duryodhana accepts him and treats him with honour, and becomes his friend. The Pandavas use every opportunity to belittle and humiliate him, leading to an enmity between Karna and the Pandavas.

Kunti, though she knows Karna is her son, never divulges the secret while he is alive.

On the eve of the great battle, Kunti reveals the secret of his birth to Karna, and then asks him to join the Pandavas. She tries to tempt him with the Kingdom. As the eldest of all, he would be the ruler of the Kingdom.

But Karna remains steadfast in his friendship but promises his mother that he would not kill four of his brothers, he will kill Arjuna or get killed by Arjuna. Thus, Kunti will still be the mother of five sons.

Karna is a generous, large-hearted man, and he makes Kunti promise not to reveal the secret of his birth as long as he is alive, as that would make the Pandavas hesitate in the battle.

He knows this will lead to certain death for him, but he accepts that and thus Karna goes to his death for the sake of friendship.

Karna is the tragic hero of the Mahabharata, whom everyone who reads the Mahabharata loves.

Krishna is, in a way, the main protagonist of the story, an avatar of Vishnu. He is born to establish Dharma. He supports the Pandavas and is the guiding force behind their victories.

When all seems lost, Krishna steps in and saves the day. The Pandavas are just instruments. Krishna is the actual doer in the story.

Krishna is one of the most popular gods in India even today. He is charming, wily, and ruthless when required. He is focused on the goal and in the Bhagavad Gita; he expounds on life and its meaning.

The Mahabharata is full of twists and turns and finally reaches a climax in the eighteen-day war in which most of the warriors meet their end.

The Pandavas finally have their victory, but it is a hollow victory as they have lost all their kith and kin, including their children.

A forgotten hero. Yuyutsu from The Mahabharata

The Mahabharata is unlike any other story in the world. It has a huge number of characters.

Just like our country, which teems with people, the Mahabharata teems with so many interesting characters.

This enormous cast of characters means that many interesting characters miss out on their due.

We all know of that mesmerizing figure of the Mahabharata, Karna, the tragic hero ever in search of his identity.

Karna strides across the Mahabharata as a colossus and he is a very attractive character drawn with a lot of love and care and then embellished by later writers.

But there was another character who is silent to a large extent and but who faces somewhat similar conditions while growing up but takes a different path.

Gandhari was pregnant for a long time, and a maid Sugadha used to look after the blind king, Dhritarashtra.

Now men have their needs and they have their ways of justifying the transgressions they do to satisfy these needs. If a woman were to do it, she would be denounced.

Dhritarashtra needed an outlet for his lust, and there was the maid Sugadha available, and the King had a liaison with her.

By the time Gandhari delivered her children, Sugadha was also pregnant, and in due course, gave birth to a healthy child, Yuyutsu.

Yuyutsu was born around the same time as Duryodhana and Bhima. Though younger to both, he was elder to the rest of the Kauravas and the Pandavas.

He was acknowledged as the son of Dhritarashtra and brought up in the palace with the Kauravas.

Like Vidur, who was Dhritarashtra's half-brother and the son of a maid, Yuyutsu was a man of high morals firmly attached to Dharma.

But unlike Vidur, who remained loyal to his half-brother or Vikarna, his Kaurava half-brother who remained loyal to Duryodhana, Yuyutsu remained steadfast to Dharma.

He was attached to his eldest cousin, Yudhishtra, who trusted him implicitly.

He helped Vidur in protecting the Pandavas from the schemes launched by Duryodhana to harm the Pandavas.

Yuyutsu was also a great warrior, acknowledged as Maharathi. The Kauravas had only 11 such warriors.

Yuyutsu had a difficult time as the stepbrother of the Kauravas. The Kauravas did not trust him and he was always at the receiving end of some humiliation or the other from them.

All his father's love seemed reserved only for Duryodhana. His mother was a lowly maid, and he is often called a Vaishyaputra or Dasiputra in some versions. He was the odd man out.

When the Pandavas came to Hastinapur after the death of their father, he was caught between what was right and being loyal to his family and his half brothers

He tries his best to get the Kauravas, especially Duryodhana, to give up his animosity and jealousy of the Pandavas but is rebuffed.

Finally, when the war is about to begin, Yuyutsu has had enough and he joins the Pandavas.

Unlike Bhishma, Drona, and many others on the Kaurava side who knowingly fight what they know to be an unrighteous war, Yuyutsu remains true to himself and his convictions.

He fights on the Pandava side, knowing both friends and foes alike would condemn him for abandoning his family at a crucial time, but he remains true to his conscience.

He is one of the few to survive the war and is part of the administrative setup at Indraprastha.

Later, as the Pandavas forsake their kingdom to go to the Himalayas at the end of their life, Yuyutsu is made the regent by Yudhhistra.

Parikshit, the son of Abhimanyu, is crowned the king, but Yuyutsu is left in charge as Parikshit is still a child.

Yuyutsu vanishes from the stage after that, a silent steadfast hero who does what has to be done without the rhetoric, chest-thumping or the noise others make.

At a time where we have so many who walk on the path of personal glory and grandiose egos away from the path of right. It is good to remember this silent man who was a warrior and yet a Moral Hero, too.

A mother's' strength

As we saw earlier, many stories were added later to the Mahabharata. This is a retelling of one of them. A tale of pride before a fall. The pride of Airawat, Arjuna, and Bhima all meet their Nemesis in this tale.

The Pandavas had built a wondrous new capital, Indraprastha. Now they planned to have a grand function, a sacrifice, a yagna as it is called.

There would be kings from all over the land as guests. There would be other important dignitaries and, of course, their relatives from Hastinapur.

Their cousins the Kauravas and their supporters from Hastinapur, Bhishma their Grandsire, Drona their Guru, all would be there.

Their in-laws, the parents, and relatives of Dhrupad would be there, and so also the Yadavas led by Krishna.

This was the opportunity to shine in front of all these guests, show them that the Pandavas had arrived!

Yudhishtra was reluctant to do this on a grand scale, but Arjuna and Bhima wanted to show off how strong they were. The forest of Khandvaprasta was burned and its denizens slaughtered to build this grand city.

Then there was Draupadi, wishing to show off the power of her husbands and she convinced Yudhishtra, who besotted with his beautiful wife, could deny her nothing.

Once agreed, the three of them, Draupadi, Arjuna, and Bhima, took charge of the arrangements.

They had completed everything on a grand scale, now they wished to have something unique to make the event stand out.

It was then that Arjuna hit upon the idea of asking his divine father, Indra, for his elephant Airawat to welcome the guests at the entrance.

Now Airawat was no ordinary elephant. He was Indra's' personal mount, a war elephant, the king of elephants, immortal and untameable by anybody except Indra.

Arjuna asked his father, Indra, for a loan of Airawat to the Pandavas for the event.

Indra was not happy. Airawat was a friend, not just an animal. He was not just a war mount, but a fellow warrior who fought and protected him in battles.

But Arjuna was dear to him and so he spoke to Airawat and Airawat agreed to go if Arjuna or his brothers came and could tame and lead him back to Earth on their own. They were to use their strengths and not seek the support of anyone else.

Arjuna agreed to the conditions and on a designated day, the Pandavas made ready to bring Airawat down from Indraloka, the celestial city high in the sky.

An enormous crowd had gathered to see this wonder.

Kunti and Draupadi were there too, so was Krishna visiting the Pandavas, his cousins.

Kunti was not happy to bring the divine and majestic Airawat down and making him welcome the guests. She expressed her unhappiness to

Krishna, who smiled his charming, enigmatic smile and asked her to be patient.

Arjuna looked around, yes there was a large audience for him to show off.

Arjuna took out his great bow the Gandiva and twanged the string, its sound clear and sharp. His hands were a blur. The greatest archer in the world displayed his sublime skills. Arrows shot out in a never-ending stream and soon they formed steps, a stairway to heaven.

As Arjuna basked in the awe of the people and the adoring admiration in Draupadi's eyes, Bhima stepped forward.

Bhima was proud of Arjuna and he did not doubt that the stairway would bear him. He hefted his mighty Gada and started the long climb to Indraloka.

Airawat was waiting. He had a lot of soma juice, that divine intoxicating drink of gods. It freed him from inhibitions and increased his strength.

He stood at the entrance of Indraloka, his eyes red with rage at the temerity of a mere mortal. He swayed back and forth, whipping up his anger.

The Gods watched in silence, wondering what would be the outcome.

Bhima stepped out of the stairway; the long climb seemed to have only warmed him up. He was a giant, an imposing man with his Gada, a mace on his shoulder.

He walked calmly up to a watchful Airawat, not frightened of the Elephant.

As soon as he was within reach, Airawat grabbed Bhima in his trunk and squeezed. The Gods gasped and Vayu Bhima's divine father was fearful for the safety of his son.

But Bhima caught the sensitive tip of the elephant's trunk and squeezed it with his considerable strength. Airawat squealed in pain and let Bhima go.

Bhima dropped to the ground and swung his mace and hit Airawat in the middle of his forehead.

The Soma juice had already given Airawat a headache. The blow rang in his head and he could not bear it. He stumbled to his knees. As he got up, Bhima cuffed him behind his ears wagging his finger, admonishing Airawat.

The Elephant, so proud of his strength, had met its match. Airawat submitted to Bhima, and a proud Bhima led him away.

The people below gasped as Bhima appeared high with Airawat in tow.

Bhima, head in the air with pride, stepped hard and ponderously down the stairway of arrows.

Arjuna basked in the adulation of all. He looked at Draupadi. "See, no other person in the world could have built such a stairway, and no one but brother Bhima could have tamed Airawat!"

Krishna smiled and then, unknown to the others, caused a small feather to fall from the sky, a feather of Garuda, the celestial eagle, the devotee of Vishnu.

The feather fell on the bridge, and it swayed. Bits of it fell. It could not bear the weight of the feather.

Bhima was holding on for dear life, Airawat was trumpeting harshly in fear and anger.

Arjuna took out his bow and shot arrow after arrow to strengthen the steps, but they shook and bigger pieces fell.

An enormous piece fell from just below Bhima's feet and he tumbled and fell from that great height.

Head over heels fell Bhima and nothing could save him felt the crowd of shouting people. Arjuna was bellowing, Draupadi crying and screaming. Krishna stood aside, smiling.

Kunti rushed forward and as the great Bhima fell, Kunti his mother reached out with her arms and caught him safely. Bhima had his eyes closed and was prepared to meet his death. He felt the gentle arms around him, holding him safe as they did during his childhood. He opened his eyes, looking in wonder at this small, frail woman who had caught him and saved him so easily. Kunti put him down gently.

Kunti stepped near to the stairs. She held it steady and Airawat stepped down and bowed to her in reverence.

The Pandavas learnt their lesson. They did not humiliate Airawat; they worshiped him and let him return to Indraloka rather than make him stand and welcome the kings who came.

The Pandavas stood at the entrance and welcomed their guests with folded hands, humility in their eyes.

A Second Chance

The Aithihyamala is a collection of folktales of Kerala compiled by Kottarathil Sankunni nearly a century ago.

One story is of one raja of Kottayam.

The royal family of Kottayam, known for its erudite and scholarly members, was a Principality located south of Cochin.

In this family was born a dunce, and he was the eldest! The Queen mother was attached to the child, but at her wit's end how to ensure that he grew up wise and good enough to rule.

The Queen arranged for many teachers famous for their knowledge and experience to tutor the boy, but they all failed and the boy was called a dunce, a clown prince derogatorily by the people.

Meanwhile, the ruler of Kozhikode, the Zamorin, had died, and the Queen needed to send someone to Kozhikode (Calicut) for a condolence visit.

As the eldest and heir apparent, the foolish prince had to be sent, and the queen was in a quandary.

The communication between the royals in those days was in a dialect of Sanskrit called the Geervanabhasha. Our prince could barely speak his mother tongue Malayalam, leave alone Sanskrit.

The harried Queen then taught the prince three words "Mayaa kim karthavyyam".

This meant what can I do for you? They instructed the prince to say these three words and nothing else. The Queen hoped that this would hide the truth from everyone.

Day and night the Queen sat and taught the sixteen-year-old prince these three words till he became perfect in their pronunciation.

During the long journey to Kozhikode also the tutors sent with the prince coached and made him practice.

They reached Kozhikode on a humid and hot day. Dark clouds were on the horizon as the monsoon was about to start.

They were received warmly and took the prince and his entourage to their chambers in the Zamorin's palace.

The prince had a bath in the royal pond and, after prayers, started off to meet the heir apparent to the Zamorin. Being a matrilineal lineage, the nephew of the departed Zamorin was his heir.

The prince was terrified. He was a simple soul, and the grand palace unnerved him. His mind was blank, and it was with fear he entered the meeting hall.

The heir apparent, dressed in his formal robes, at waiting for the prince.

The prince moved forward and, folding his hands in greeting, saying, "Khim mama karthavyyam?" Which meant what is my duty?

The Zamorin's heir was startled and annoyed and he sarcastically replied "Dheerghoucharanam karthavyyam". Which meant proper pronunciation is your duty.

The audience ended in laughter from the people gathered there. The Kottayam retinue felt embarrassed by their foolish prince. They immediately withdrew from the audience and started back home with a dejected prince.

Once they reached Kottayam, they appraised the Queen of the humiliation.

The Queen could no longer be in doubt, a fool could not be the ruler and in sorrow, she ordered that the poor prince be thrown from the top of the sacred waterfall the Kumaradhara.

Early morning, the poor prince was bathed and dressed in his royal robes. The Queen could not bear to see her eldest born son being thrown to sure death. But she had no choice, for the good of her kingdom she felt she had to do this. The prince's siblings wailed and tried to stop the Queen. Everyone tried to stop the Queen. The prince, though a fool, was a simple, cheerful soul loved by everyone.

But the Queen was determined. She said I love him but my duty to the Kingdom comes first. I pray to the Gods that they save and return my son to me as an intelligent man. It is said in the ancient legends that if he survives the fall, he would return as an intelligent man.

The soldiers tied the prince's hands and legs and threw him from the top of the raging falls. The monsoon was in full swing and the water gushed and fell with a roar from a height of 70 feet.

The rushing waters carried the poor prince, and he surrendered to the flow, praying to God. The waters carried him and dropped him on the rocks below. The prince was battered and bruised, but miraculously alive.

He lay unconscious under the heavy pounding waters for hours till some soldiers searching for his body found him.

The Queen and the kingdom felt great joy in finding the prince alive. They took him to the palace and cared for him. When he regained consciousness, he was a changed man. The Gods had answered the queen. They had saved and infused him with new vigour and intelligence.

The Queen arranged for the best tutors in the land and within six months; the prince was as knowledgeable as any of them.

The prince not only became a good ruler, but also a great poet. He became famous as the author of Attakathakal, which means stories for dance. They use his compositions even today in Kathakali dramas. He is known as Kottayathu Raja or Kottayathu Thampuran and his plays are still staged by Kathakali artists today and are very popular with the audience centuries after he wrote them.

I still remember watching the Kathakali performance of his Kalyana Sougandhikam as a small child in the temple courtyard, mesmerized at the story of a besotted Bhima going in search of a flower at the behest of his wife, Panchali.

Life is like that. When you feel that you have reached the end, it gives you a second chance to become better than you ever were.

So never lose hope.

Avial and its Mahabharata connection

Avial is a mixed vegetable dish, iconic, popular and essential in a Kerala feast, the Sadhya.

In Tamil Nadu and coastal Karnataka also, it is very popular.

They make it out of a mix of vegetables, curd, and coconut, goes well with rice and today even with chapatis, puris, and bread.

It can be thick with little gravy or thinner. Most of the time, curd is also used for the gravy, but it can be made without curd as well.

In modern times, the mix has changed and you will find people adding vegetables as per their liking. Mostly the vegetables used are yam, plantain, etc, etc which are crisp and hard and do not become mushy when boiled.

The dish remains essentially the same. It can be served hot or cold, I like to have a slightly chilled avial with bread. It can be mixed with rice and used as the main dish, or eaten as a side dish.

Now you will wonder how this dish so popular is connected with the Mahabharata. This is what this story is about.

The Pandavas and Kauravas were growing up together in the palace.

The Kauravas were unhappy as they feared the loss of the kingdom to their cousins, the Pandavas. They felt the Kingdom belonged to them as their father, Dhritarashtra, was the king.

The Pandavas were unhappy, as the children of the dead king Pandu and as Yudhishtra was the eldest, they felt the kingdom should be theirs. But as fatherless children of a widowed mother, they had no power in the state councils.

This bred animosity and anger between the Pandavas and Kauravas.

Bhima was big and strong, even though not grown to full adulthood, he was bigger than most men. He delighted in bullying the Kauravas, who were no match for his strength.

He picked them up and dropped them hard on the ground and when they climbed into trees to hide from him; he shook the tree till they fell.

The Kauravas hated the Pandavas, but they hated Bhima the most.

They planned to do away with him and, knowing his love for eating, especially sweets, they fed him poisoned sweets one day.

The poison had its effect and Bhima fell; the Kauravas believed he was dead and threw him in the nearby river.

Bhima was not dead; his colossal frame caused the poison to have a reduced effect on him. But he was unconscious and deep in the river. He was on the point of death.

In the river lived the Nagas, powerful, venomous, and with knowledge of all poisons.

Kunti, Bhima's mother, was a descendent of Yadu who had married a Naga princess and thus Bhima had Naga blood in him.

The Nagas found him lying on the river bed and the recognizing him took him to their city beneath the river.

There they revived him and the great Naga king Vasuki came to meet Bhima.

"Son, you are descended from a Naga princess and are one of us," said Vasuki to Bhima. "Rest and recover your strength and we will ensure that in the future, no poison will affect you."

Bhima was happy. It was his nature to enjoy the moment and not worry too much about the future. Being with the Nagas who treated him with affection, indulged him, and gave him due importance made him happy. They also treated him so that all the poison in his body was drained and he became immune to any further attacks with poison. The Nagas restored him to full strength. In fact, he was stronger than before. It was now time to return and surprise everyone.

Meanwhile, in Hastinapur, there was consternation when Bhima did not turn up for the evening meal.

The Kauravas claimed to have seen him go towards the river; they found his clothes on the banks.

The Kauravas set it about that Bhima had gone for a swim and had been attacked by an enormous crocodile and had drowned in the river.

The Pandavas felt helpless. Without Bhima, their strength was considerably reduced. They believed the Kauravas had a hand in Bhima's disappearance, but the wise minister, Vidur, and other well-wishers advised them not to go for a confrontation now.

It was fifteen days since Bhima was missing, and they presumed he was dead.

The funerary services were being planned for Bhima and as part of it, a feast was being organized for the Brahmins and all who would come for the mourning.

It was the day when the feast was to take place. Since very early in the morning, the cooks were preparing for the required dishes to be served for a feast on such occasions. The scriptures specify dishes that should be served on such occasions.

Dawn was breaking and the Pandavas, the Kauravas, and all the men of the family were at the river for their morning bath and ritual prayers for the occasion.

The sun rose and in the morning light, Bhima rose from the waters laughing at the shocked expressions on everyone's face.

The Pandavas were beside themselves with joy. The Kauravas looked on with chagrin and dismay.

Yudhishtra advised Bhima to remain quiet and make no accusations till they consulted Vidur.

Vasuki, the Naga king, had also advised Bhima to remain quiet and bide his time.

Vidur came and listened to Bhima and advised him to follow Vasuki's advice. It would be Bhima's word against the Kaurava's word and the King would believe his sons rather than Bhima.

Vidur got up to leave. "I have to tell the royal cooks to stop their preparations for the feast."

Bhima enjoyed going into kitchens. He liked anything to do with food.

The bustling kitchen came to a halt on seeing Vidur and Bhima. It thrilled the chief cooks and the kitchen staff to see Bhima; he was a favourite who frequented the kitchen since he was a small child. Food made Bhima happy and his happiness was infectious. The people in the Kitchen loved him.

Vidur smiled to see Bhima surrounded by these smiling faces. He left quietly as a boisterous Bhima concocted a story to explain his happiness.

Bhima found that the chief cook looked a little worried and sought the reason.

"Look at all these cut vegetables. We cannot prepare the dishes planned now that you are back. They will go to waste." Said one cook.

Now Bhima himself was an excellent cook and a foodie. He empathized with cooks on a waste of food.

He thought for a while and then smiled, "Today is a new birth for me, a new beginning and I will cook something new today and see that these vegetables do not go waste."

In those days, mixing different vegetables was frowned upon and never done. But Bhima brushed aside all objections.

He mixed all the vegetables together, boiled them, added coconut and curd and a new dish, avial, was made for the first time by Bhima.

Everyone appreciated the dish and soon became so popular that it is now a must at all feasts in Kerala. It is also popular in Tamil Nadu and Coastal Karnataka.

Mothers have created the link with Bhima, the strongest man in the Mahabharata for avial to entice their children to eat vegetables. The dish is chock full of vegetables, sometimes up to 13 to fourteen different vegetables, curd or yogurt, and normally lightly spiced. A very healthy dish!

Like Bhima himself, Avial remains enduring and strong amidst all the changes it has faced and is still a favourite, much-valued dish in Kerala.

Bhima and Hanuman

As a child growing up in Mumbai, vacations were exciting times. We did not have the luxury of the internet or TV. Even the availability of books was limited. During vacations, we travelled south to Tamil Nadu and Kerala. Vacations meant listening to stories from our grandmothers and other elders. It also meant performances like Kathakali, which told us stories from our epics.

They would perform the Kathakali dance drama in the temple courtyard. The stage would be at the proper height for those who sat cross-legged in the soft sand.

The drums would beat throughout the day, and the program for the night announced.

There would be light from flickering oil lamps, the stage an open platform with swaying palms around it and the night sky as a backdrop.

The singer would start his song and drum beats would rise as the larger-than-life figures strut onto the stage. Colourful faces with swirling skirts, the actors would dance, jump and bring much-loved characters to life.

One unforgettable tale I watched was that of Bhima and Hanuman. A story that brought two favourite characters together.

This is a retelling of that magical tale that I heard and watched long ago.

Bhima was proud of his strength and arrogant about it. The Pandavas were in the forest after losing their kingdom in the game of dice.

Arjuna, the archer, was away in the sacred mountains, praying for divine weapons for the war that everyone knew was coming.

It was early morning, the sun just stretching out above the trees. Draupadi was at the river having her bath with Bhima standing guard.

There was a gentle breeze and wafting on it came the most pleasant of scents.

Draupadi looked up. The scent had refreshed her; it was like no other scent. Floating on the river waters was a flower she had never seen before.

Draupadi picked it up, yes it was the flower that had that heavenly scent.

Draupadi finished her bath and came out holding the flower in her hand. Bhima watched her with a smile. Draupadi, the royal princess of Panchala and the Queen of Indraprastha, was happy with a flower.

Bhima felt sad and happy watching her pleasure. Here was a woman brought up in luxury, Queen of an Empire, wife of five famous warriors. Yet here she was in the forest, living in a hut, clad in rough garments, wearing herself out, looking after the five of them. All because Yudhishtra could not control his gambling urge.

Draupadi came up to Bhima and held out the flower to him. He clasped the flower and her hand, and Draupadi laughed. "I wanted you to smell this flower, not hold my hand. If you can get me some more of these flowers, I can make a garland to string around the house."

Bhima smiled. "Off course, I will get you the flowers. I wish you would ask for something more difficult."

Bhima started for the forest, smiling to himself, "Me, the strongest and greatest warrior in the world going to pick flowers, how my brothers and my friends will laugh. I am more suited to catching tigers and elephants!"

But husbands, even in those days, had to please their wives.

Now Bhima was proud of his strength and enjoyed showing it off. He hefted his mace and roared out a challenge while walking through the forest.

The elephants heard him and moved away from his path. The tiger snarled in fury but slunk away and the monkeys chattered at him, but kept their distance.

Striding arrogantly, Bhima followed the scent wafting on the breeze. The forest had become thick and the path narrow.

He turned a corner on that narrow path and, lying in his way, was an old decrepit monkey.

Bhima roared out to the monkey to move out of his way, but the monkey turned its large eyes pitifully in him and whispered "I am sorry but I cannot move, I am too old".

In those days, many animals could speak with men and with each other.

Bhima thought the monkey was pretending and again shouted at it.

The monkey closed its eyes in pain and whispered, "stop that bellowing it only saps what little energy I have."

Bhima was surprised. He stood there with his mouth open. No one had ever spoken to him like this before.

The monkey opened one eye and said, "close your mouth or a fly will go in."

Bhima closed his mouth angrily and strode forward. He glared at the monkey, hoping to frighten it.

The monkey now opened both eyes, looked wearily at Bhima and whispered, "don't just stand there. If you want to move forward, jump over me and go. You are a fat fellow, but even then, you should be able to jump over me."

Bhima was angry and did not know what to do. The monkey was old and not threatening him. But how could he jump over the creature? It was much older than him. It would be a mark of disrespect and against dharma.

Bhima controlled his anger and sat down near the monkey. "Just move your tail out of the way and I will pass," requested Bhima.

The monkey seemed to strain but could not move its tail.

The monkey asked Bhima to lift and move its tail.

"I cannot touch a dirty animal like you with my hands. I will move your tail with my mace," said an exasperated Bhima.

But however much he tried, Bhima could not move that tail.

The Monkey watched in amusement and Bhima became furious.

Bhima kept aside his mace. "I will pick you up and fling you into the trees, dirty fellow," shouted an angry Bhima. It was now a matter of pride and prestige for him.

Bhima strained all his muscles. He stormed and raged, but he could not move the monkey's tail.

At last, an exhausted Bhima sat down. He was numb and his mind was empty. As anger left him, reason stepped in.

No ordinary monkey was this, realised Bhima. His pride left him and he kneeled and bowed his head.

"I am ashamed, great one. You cannot be an ordinary monkey. Please show me your true self," said Bhima.

The monkey smiled and, in an instant, changed to the stalwart figure of Hanuman.

Bhima was overcome. This was Hanuman, who was his elder brother in spirit. Both were the sons of Vayu, the wind god.

Hanuman lifted Bhima and his touch refreshed Bhima. All his tiredness left him.

For a time, the two brothers sat together, sharing thoughts. Bhima's heart was full of happiness and love. His pride had vanished with Hanuman's touch. He realised the need to respect everyone and not use his strength to bully the weak. That was the actual mark of a powerful person.

Hanuman smiled at him, "now you have become truly strong. Wait here. I will get you the flowers. As a mortal, you cannot get them."

Hanuman returned with the flowers. He blessed Bhima. "Tell your brothers not to worry. Tell Arjuna I will be on his flag and be with him in his battles in the great war that is coming. And when you, my Bhima, shout your battle cry, my voice will join in and your opponents will be in fear," said Hanuman.

A refreshed Bhima quickly returned with the flowers. His brothers and Draupadi heard his tale, and it filled their hearts with gratitude and love for Hanuman. It filled them with new hope and looked forward to the future.

Hanuman is strong, but also wise and compassionate. He protects all who pray to him and that is why even today people pray to him when in difficulties. The Hanuman Chalisa, a hymn in praise of Hanuman, is sung in homes all over India with belief and devotion, seeking Hanuman's grace and protection.

Ganesh and Ravana

The Lord of Lanka Ravana was a great bhakta of Lord Shiva. He was also a powerful king who had subjugated many rulers, and the Devas, the celestial lesser gods, were frightened of him.

One day Ravana travelled to Kailasa, the abode of Shiva, and prayed to him.

Ravana not only wanted to have a darshan of Shiva, he wanted to get Shiva to materialize the Atma Linga and give it to him to take to Lanka.

Now, this Linga would make Ravana more powerful. When they realized this, the Devas were worried. The Atma Linga, an embodiment of Shiva, gave strength to those who worshipped it.

When Shiva materialized it, the Devas wanted the Linga to worship, so that they could gain strength.

Ravana was meditating, performing austerities, and praying to Shiva. The Devas were frightened of Ravana and did not dare try to disturb him or break his prayers.

They also knew that Shiva did not bother about the social mores or what the Devas thought or wanted. If a devotee prayed genuinely, Shiva would grant him what the devotee aspired for.

Ravana was a genuine devotee, who worshiped and prayed to Shiva daily. Shiva would definitely grant him darshan.

How do you get a man to do what you want? You seek his wife's help!

The Devas gathered around Parvathi, Siva's consort. They prostrated themselves in front of her and refused to get up till she promised to help.

That evening, when they were alone, Parvathi explained to Shiva the worries of the Devas.

Shiva smiled and said, "Ravana is a genuine devotee. I cannot deny him his prayers. All he wants is a symbol of me to worship."

Parvati did not agree. "Yes, I know Ravana is devoted to you and you cannot deny him his desire to worship you. But he is also arrogant and will use the strength he gains to harass the Devas; he will be uncontrollable."

Shiva mused over this. "Yes, you are, as always, right, my dear wife. The only way out is that you put this problem to our son Ganesha. He will know what to do."

The Devas, when they heard this, felt reassured. Ganesha was a calm person who addressed every issue with his intellect. They worshipped him as the remover of obstacles and the Devas were confident, but wondered how he would do it, as he was unconventional in his ways.

Ganesha agreed readily to the request from his mother and waved the Devas away when they wanted to know how he would fight and overcome the fearsome Ravana.

Reluctantly, they offered to become his army in the war against Ravana.

Ganesha brushed them off, saying, "War is not the option always, violence is a circle that needs to be avoided. Now that you have laid the problem before me, I will resolve it. You may go back to your homes."

The Devas had no other option but to go away after this. They hoped Ganesha would resolve the problem without them having to fight with Ravana.

Shiva finally appeared before Ravana, happy at the success of his prayers.

Shiva smiled at him and said, "I know what you want, Ravana, but you need to ask for it."

Ravana bowed and replied, "Oh lord, please give me a symbol that has a part of you which I can take to Lanka and worship."

Shiva looked at Ravana, enigmatically.

"I will grant you the request Ravana, I will give you an Atma Linga to worship. But there is a condition: you must carry it to Lanka without keeping it on the earth anywhere. Wherever you keep it on the ground, the Linga will get fixed there. You should also go back the same way that you have come. You cannot now call for your pushpaka vimana or any help from Lanka."

Now Lanka was thousands of kilometres away, Ravana had walked all the way alone as part of his prayer.

Now walking back carrying the Linga would require tremendous focus and strength. But Ravana was confident and proud of his strength. He blithely agreed.

Carrying the Atma Linga was not a problem, it was small enough. Ravana set off on his long journey.

He would not stop; he did not want to stop. If he ate, he would have to stop. And if he stopped, the Devas might attack him, and though he could defeat them, one of them would be sly and quick enough to steal the Linga.

Now that would not do. If someone stole and put the Linga down, then Ravana would lose the Linga.

So, Ravana started walking without stopping for food, without sleeping all those thousands of kilometres.

You can survive without food, but everyone needs water to survive. Especially when you are walking and the sun beats down on you.

Ravana was no exception. He sipped a little water from his kamandal now and then.

Days became nights and then a week and Ravana had hit a rhythm and was walking steadily and strongly. He had crossed the hot central plains and was now on the southern coast.

There was lush greenery around, swaying coconut palms, spreading shades of mango and jackfruit, sparkling brooks, and the sea seen now and then.

It was a beautiful land with friendly people who recognized the great King that he was.

Now Ravana was a popular King, his people loved him, he was a brilliant scholar well versed in all subjects. He took care of the common people. He was a fair and wise ruler.

The problem with Ravana was his ego, his belief that because he was strong, he could do anything he wanted. This pride led him into actions that were against the dharma. In his pride and anger, he could do the vilest of acts. The man killed people. He carried away the wives or daughters of others; he took away other people's belongings if he felt like it.

But to the common people, this was not obvious. He did not harm them and he took care of their welfare.

So it was that as the people watched him striding along, they stopped their work and waved out to him.

The rains were imminent, dark clouds were gathering and then the first drops of rain fell. The land welcomed the life-giving drops of water, and there was the heady aroma of the earth after the first rains.

Ravana felt refreshed by the cooling drops of water. He walked through the rain, through the slush, gripping his feet.

He knew he was near to his home. A few more days and he would be in Lanka.

The rains had stopped. It was pleasant now, the leaves green with drops of water glistening, the cool wind, and the pleasant people around. Victory was just around the corner.

Ravana lost his focus, he relaxed, and Ganesh, following his progress smiled, the opportunity was at hand.

Ravana had just reached Gokarna, a small village in Karnataka. A beautiful place with an abundance of nature all around. It did not have too many people, and those whom Ravana could see were simple folks going about their work.

Now that he had relaxed, his body intruded. The rains and the constant diet of water meant that his bladder was full, and he needed to empty it.

Each step was agony. The urge to release the water inside him was strong and clouded his brain. The urge grew and, as we all know, this is an urge almost impossible to control beyond a limit.

Now Ravana could not urinate holding the sacred Linga. He considered that a base act. He was desperate and in agony.

There was a boy grazing cattle nearby.

The boy looked innocent and cherubic; he did not seem very intelligent. Ravana felt he could trust the boy to not take away the Linga and run. Also, no Deva would appear looking so dumb, their egos would come in their way.

He asked the boy to hold the Linga, which the boy refused. After a great deal of persuasion and the promise of a valuable jewel, the boy agreed reluctantly.

But the boy had a condition. He would call out Ravana's name three times, and if Ravana did not come, he would put the Linga down.

A desperate Ravana agreed. He felt he could easily come back before the boy called his name three times. As you can see, his urge had clouded his brain.

Ravana turned around to relive himself and the boy called out Ravana's name three times quickly in one breath.

As an aghast Ravana turned around, the boy calmly put the Lingam down.

An enraged Ravana caught hold of the boy, whose eyes now shone with intelligence and calmness.

Ravana was beside himself with anger and he clouted the boy on his head with his fist.

But Ravana restrained himself from doing anything further. This was a young Shepherd boy and not a warrior. He had given fair warning that he would keep the Lingam down.

So, Ravana refrained from doing any further harm to the boy. The boy was, of course, not any Deva but Ganesha.

Seeing Ravana controlling himself and also knowing how much Ravana was attached to his father Shiva, Ganesha accepted the knock on his head without retaliation.

Ganesh resumed his normal appearance. Ravana looked at him and smiled wryly. "I should have known the Devas would get someone else to do their dirty work."

Ravana bent to offer his salutations to Ganesha and tried to lift the Atma Linga again.

Ravana used all his strength and knowledge, but he could not shift or move the Linga.

The Linga slowly sank into the ground and even today when you go to the Gokarna temple, the Lingam is underground and you cannot see it. If you put your hand inside the hole in the rock, you can feel the Atma Lingam. Because even such a mighty king like Ravana could not shift it, the Gokarna temple is called the Mahabaleshwara Temple. Which means the strongest lord.

A dejected Ravana accepted the situation and realized his pride and ego had come in the way of his success. But being Ravana, he did not change himself. He shrugged his mighty shoulders, urged his tired body to move, and started his long walk back home to Lanka.

Ganesha watched him go. He had accomplished what he needed to do.

But Ganesha had accepted the knock on his head and today the Ganesha at the Gokarna temple still has a dent on his head.

Ganesha and the Moon

It was Ganesh Chaturthi, and the world was celebrating this auspicious day.

Ganesha was happy, but also a bit hassled. He had so many invitations. He did not want to disappoint any of his well-wishers, so he tried to accept the maximum he could.

Everywhere he went, his devotees had made his favourite foods, especially the modak in its different versions.

Ganesha finally called it a day. Even he was satiated with all the food he had, and it was late at night now.

Ganesha mounted his Vahan, the mouse who was dozing off, dreaming of food. The mouse was also full of the food offered by Ganesha's devotees.

Ganesha shook his mouse awake. The mouse woke up reluctantly; he was having the most wonderful dream of being inside a modak and eating his way out. With a sigh, he accepted Ganesha sitting astride him and started the long walk home.

The moon was watching the little mouse carrying a well-fed Ganesha with amusement.

Both Ganesha and the mouse were not very alert, and the moon decided to have some fun at Ganesha's expense.

The moon was not worried about playing a trick on Ganesha that would make him angry, as Ganesha was very laid back, very intelligent, never lost his temper and had a good sense of humour.

So just as the mouse with a dozing Ganesha reached near a tree, the moon hid behind a cloud.

The darkness and sleepiness made the mouse stumble and fall over a tree root. A dozing Ganesha also rolled down.

Ganesha sat up leaning against the tree and the mouse, too, rolled upright.

They both heard loud laughter and looked up to see the moon laughing at their expense.

Ganesha was upset. He had been woken up suddenly and rudely. The moon laughing irritated him further.

"Oh, it was so funny to see you riding that mouse and even funnier to see you rolling down," said the moon, laughing loudly.

The mouse gave Ganesha an injured look.

Ganesha was exasperated. The moon was adding insult to injury.

He looked up angrily and said, "You are having fun at our expense, well if anyone worships or even looks at you, they will be falsely blamed and accused."

The moon was very proud of his looks and enjoyed people looking up at him in admiration. Now on he would be ignored and all the focus would be on Ganesha. He pleaded with Ganesha to remove the curse.

Ganesha realised that for once he had let emotions get the better of his intellect. But he could not remove the curse. But he could modify it a bit, so he stipulated the curse would take effect only on Ganesh Chaturthi day.

So, on Ganesh Chaturthi, they expect us to focus on Ganesha and ignore the moon, however bright and beautiful the moon is.

Actions that we take in anger are many a time actions which we regret later.

The moon realised that laughing at someone's physical attributes or laughing at others' misfortune could cause enmity and misfortune for us, too.

Even now on Ganesh Chaturthi, people believe that looking at the moon brings bad luck.

Hanuman's devotion

Rama returned to Ayodhya with Sita after winning the war with Ravana. Vibhishana, Ravana's brother, was crowned the king of Lanka.

The citizens of Ayodhya were happy that their prince has come back and that too after a grand victory over the powerful king of Lanka

Rama's coronation as the king of Ayodhya was planned on a grand scale and attended by all the kings from near and far

The powerful vanaras, their stalwart king Sugreeva, were the cynosure of all eyes.

But everyone wanted to have a look at Hanuman, the hero who had so many victories to credit.

There were so many stories of Hanuman, his strength, his sagacity, his knowledge, and wisdom.

But they rarely saw Hanuman. He was happiest serving Rama, and that is what he did. He looked after all that Rama required.

Rama's brothers were jealous of Hanuman. Bharat, Laxman and Shatrughan also wanted to serve Rama and be with him.

But they were consoled with the thought that once the coronation was over, Hanuman would leave with the other vanaras

The coronation was over and everyone had left. But Hanuman was still there, ever at Rama's side and in his service.

He brought the water in the morning for Rama to wash and clean his face; he set out Rama's clothes; he fixed and set up Rama's work for the day.

He arranged Rama's food, accompanied Rama on his visits and inspections.

When Rama came back tired, Hanuman was there to press his tired feet, feed him nourishing food. In return, he asked for nothing.

Rama's brothers were getting impatient and jealous. They wanted to serve Rama, but they all also loved Hanuman. They hesitated to tell him and wondering how to let Hanuman know their mind.

At last, Bharat hit upon an idea. They made a schedule of all the work that was there to be done for Rama. They allocated it among themselves, leaving out Hanuman, and prepared a royal order of the same.

They pleaded with Sita for her for help and to get the royal order signed by Rama.

Sita was very fond of Hanuman and hesitated, but she was also very fond of Laxman, Bharat, and Shatrughan. She agreed to help.

That night, she presented the royal order with the schedule to Rama.

Rama read it and smiled. "Are you and my brothers sure you want to do this? You have left Hanuman out of this schedule," Rama asked Sita.

"Yes, we are sure. Hanuman will be disappointed, but will understand," Sita replied.

Rama laughed, "you don't understand Hanuman and you are underestimating him," said Rama and signed the order.

The next day morning when Hanuman came to wake up Rama, he found Laxman, Bharat, and Shatrughan there at the door.

They silently handed over the royal order and waited for Hanuman to protest. But Hanuman smiled and asked gently, "can I do any service that is not mentioned here?"

The three brothers laughed. "Yes, let us know what service you wish to do and we will add it,". said Bharat

The brothers were confident that there was no service that Hanuman could offer. They had covered all the services.

Hanuman smiled innocently. "When Lord Rama yawns, I will snap my fingers so that no evil befalls him," said Hanuman.

The three brothers laughingly agreed and thought inwardly Hanuman was a vanara, so he has chosen foolishly. They took the changed order to Sita for Rama's signature and seal.

Sita, too, laughed at the choice made by Hanuman. She took the order to Rama and, giving it to him, said, "Hanuman is so innocent. He is like a child. See what service he has had to choose, and he is happy with it."

Rama signed the order and smiled at Sita and told her, "Hanuman is the most intelligent person I know, yes he is innocent and humble, but never underestimate him."

Sita laughed at that, saying, "you will always take the side of your favourite devotee."

She took the order and gave it to the waiting brothers and Hanuman. As soon as Hanuman saw the order, he happily rushed into the room and took his place in front of Rama, looking up adoringly at Rama's face.

It surprised the others, but Rama told them, "How will Hanuman know when I will yawn? So, he has to watch me all the time."

Rama laughed at the consternation, surprise, and dismay on the faces of Sita, Laxman, Bharat, and Shatrughan. Hanuman had effortlessly managed what he wanted the most, be with Rama always.

Throughout that day, while the others rushed around doing the various jobs that were required, Hanuman sat comfortably in front of Rama, looking up at him. Hanuman accompanied Rama everywhere. He rode in the chariot with Rama; he sat opposite him during all meals; he was with Rama every minute watching for Rama to yawn.

Bharat, Laxman, and Shatrughan now realised how much work Hanuman had been doing earlier, all alone, just so that he could be with Rama.

It was night, and it was time now for Rama and Sita to retire for the night.

Entering the bedroom, it startled Sita to find Hanuman sitting at the bottom of the bed. She asked him to go out. But he refused.

"Mother Sita, it is night time and Rama will yawn more and so I need to be here to snap my fingers," said Hanuman.

Sita was furious, and she turned to Rama for support, but Rama told her, "This was your doing along with my brothers. I did what you wanted, so now you must resolve it."

Sita stormed out and called Laxman, Bharat, and Shatrughan. The four of them pleaded with Hanuman to not be in the room.

Hanuman was large-hearted and generous; Sita and Rama's brothers were also beloved to him. He agreed to remain outside the bedroom.

Heaving a sigh of relief, Sita and the others retired for the night.

Hanuman went to his room, but he was in a dilemma. How would he be able to do his duty? So, he returned and climbed up onto the balcony of Rama's room. He curled himself up comfortably and waited expectantly to hear Rama yawning.

But the night was filled with other sounds, an owl hooting, dogs barking or howling, the night watchman calling out his warning. Hanuman was now worried. What if he missed hearing Rama yawn amidst all this, and also sometimes yawns made no sound?

Hanuman then hit on an idea. He would keep snapping his fingers so that if Rama yawned, there would be no missing any yawn.

So, Hanuman snapped his fingers, first one hand, then the other. He set up a pleasant rhythm and moved to it; he was happy. Faster and faster, he snapped, eyes closed, contemplating on Lord Rama.

Inside the room, Rama yawned. He could not stop. He yawned faster and faster. Rama was looking tired, ready to sleep, but he could not. He was now yawning continuously, faster, ever faster till at last his mouth would not close.

An alarmed Sita raised the alarm. Bharat, Laxman, and Shatrughan came running. They stood there, aghast. Bharat was wise enough to understand and immediately sent Shatrughan to call Hanuman. Only he could resolve this.

Hanuman was not in his room and Shatrughan searched high and low but could not find him. He came and reported to Bharat.

Sita, wise in the ways of Hanuman, realised he would be somewhere nearby. She opened the balcony door and there was Hanuman, happily snapping his fingers and chanting Rama's name.

She called out to him and asked him to come inside. Still chanting Rama's name, snapping and moving to the beat, Hanuman entered and saw Rama.

He stopped snapping, and Rama closed his mouth, but looked exhausted.

Sita and Rama's brothers understood the devotion of Hanuman. They also realised that the Lord is bound to his devotees. Once they are devoted to him, he also is as attached to them and nothing can break that bond.

Karna and Arjuna

The Mahabharata is one of our greatest stories. Over the years, they have added many tales to the major story of a great war fought between two factions of a family.

These tales add to the flavour of the epic and embellish the characters. This is one such story.

Arjuna was always jealous of Karna. Karna was handsome, dignified, a great warrior renowned for his valour and archery skills. But the one thing that marked Karna out was his generosity.

Karna came from a poor background and did not have the advantages of privilege that Arjuna had as a Kuru prince. Karna had come up the hard way and always had empathy towards the people in need.

Karna had been crowned the King of Anga, which was a small kingdom as compared to the vast empire ruled by the Pandavas from Indraprastha, their capital.

The charity given by the Pandavas was thus many times what Karna could give, and yet Karna was called the Dhanveer. The generous hero.

Krishna was Arjuna's close friend; he was also Karna's friend.

One day while walking together Arjuna was cribbing about the unfairness of life.

Arjuna was especially peeved, with Karna being called the most generous person around.

Krishna smiled mischievously and taught Arjuna a practical lesson.

He, with his Maya, created a mountain of gold in a nearby village and asked Arjuna to ensure all of it was given to the villagers. Arjuna was to ensure that all the gold was given and not keep anything for himself.

Arjuna walked around the village with a crier beating drums announcing that he would distribute gold to all of them and they would have to report near the mountain with the proof of being residents of that village.

The villagers were in ecstasy; they sang praises of Arjun and the Pandavas and followed him to the Mountain.

Arjuna swelled with pride at hearing the praises of the people, and he dug and give large portions of gold to the villagers.

Gold can generate greed. It is its inherent property. The best of men or women get seduced by the lure of Gold.

The villagers were no exception; they collected the Gold, deposited it in their houses and came back and again stood in line to collect some more.

Old men barely able to walk, young toddlers, high-born ladies, the common folk, warriors, brahmins, farmers everyone rushed to collect the gold.

Arjuna was hard at work, digging out the Gold, distributing what he thought was a fair share to people. But the more he dug, the mountain grew. It did not diminish.

Arjuna was loth to leave the mountain even during the night as he was worried someone would steal the gold.

The people also kept coming back, and they kept poor Arjuna busy day and night.

After two days and nights, even Arjuna was exhausted. He pleaded with Krishna to help him. Smiling his enigmatic smile, Krishna made the mountain go away. The people returned to the village now that there was no gold.

Krishna took Arjuna to another nearby village and created a similar mountain of gold. He called Karna to the village.

He told Karna, "Please distribute all this gold to these villagers". This time, he did not even specify that Karna should keep nothing.

Karna called the village headman and some of the other elders. He pointed at the mountain of Gold and told them, "This is for all you in the village, do with it as you want" and waved off their gratitude walked off without bothering to even go into the village to receive their adulation and praises.

Krishna smiled at Arjuna. "now do you understand?" he asked. "Karna is an enlightened soul not caring for material gain, especially that which he has not earned. He also does not care about praises from anyone or what they say about him."

Arjuna was downcast. Krishna patted him "my dear Arjun, you wanted the people to praise you, you gave to get those praises. The gold also attracted you, hence you called each villager and were distributing the gold as if it were yours."

"I did not tell Karna he cannot keep any of the gold. I only told him to distribute the gold to the villagers."

"Karna heard me, understood what I wanted, and did not have the smallest hesitation to give the Gold."

A crestfallen Arjun now understood the lesson Krishna had taught him.

Ravana and Mahabali

Multiverse is the flavour of the day and Marvel's Multiverse movies are all the rage. But the multiverse is not a new idea, it existed in Indian Mythology for ages. There are many stories where characters from one epic land in another. There are multiple worlds and many versions. Reincarnation itself is somewhat of a multiverse idea.

There is a little-known story about Mahabali and Ravana, which is an example of this. My retelling of the story goes like this.

Ravana was at the height of his power. He was the lord of all he surveyed. He was bored. Power had gone to his head and good sense had fled.

An idle mind is the devil's workshop, they say.

Ravana's mind was in idle mode, and he was ripe for any mischief.

He wanted to shake the world and let them know his power. He wondered what he should do.

He then remembered the great king Mahabali, the grandson of Prahalad, the favourite of Vishnu.

Bali was now languishing in Patal, sent there by a perfidious Vishnu. Ravana raged at the injustice and determined that he needed to rescue Bali. Once he rescued Bali, he would set Bali up as one of his vassals. He then would be known as Maha Ravana, the rescuer of Mahabali.

Ravana travelled to the 4th planet in the Patal universe where he was told Bali lived.

He found it to be a rich world, a planet of peace and goodwill. Ravana was surprised; he expected Bali to be in a world full of trouble and despair. He asked the first person he met about Bali.

The person smile; "you are asking about our ruler, Mahabali? He lives in that palace at the top of the hill."

Ravana was surprised. He had expected Bali to be a prisoner or in dire straits, eager to be rescued.

But we are set in our ways. Ravana was convinced that Bali was a prisoner and required rescue. He strode forth to the palace gate.

He announced himself in a stentorian voice. There was no response. Ravana stood outside the palace gate. It was the middle of the afternoon and very hot. He again shouted, but there was no response. There was no one around except for a lazy dog sleeping nearby who opened one eye and gave Ravana a baleful look.

Ravana was becoming angry, and he hated dogs. He used his mace to bang on the massive gates. There was no response from within, but the dog gave a snarl.

Ravana turned toward the dog and lifted his mace, the dog stood up and showed its teeth menacingly.

Ravana was in a quandary. It was beneath him to get into a brawl with a mere dog. What would people think? But the dog showed no fear and stood its ground. It was growling now.

There was the sound of bolts being drawn, a welcome sound to Ravana. The dog lay down again and Ravana turned to the gate.

There was a dwarf at the gate holding a small club. The dwarf did not speak but raised his eyebrows in query.

Ravana, now in a rage at this unceremonious welcome, stated his name and his purpose.

The dwarf shook his head and started to close the gate. Ravana jumped to smash the dwarf, the gate, and everything with his mace.

The dwarf negligently raised his club, and Ravana's blow was arrested. Try as he might, Ravana could not force his way past the dwarf.

The dwarf looked at him with a smile, not saying a word. Ravana used his maya, his powers of magic and deception. He grew in size and raised his foot to stamp the dwarf and found the dwarf had also grown to an equal size.

He became invisible, but the dwarf could still see and stop him. Ravana became tiny. He thought he could slip through in his microscopic size. A large foot came down on Ravana. The dwarf had seen Ravana and caught him under his foot.

Ravana struggled, he raged. He bit and scratched, but could not escape. He could not grow back to his normal size. He felt helpless. Tired and drained of all his vaunted energy, Ravana lay weeping like a child.

The dwarf picked him up, patted him gently, and wiped his tears. The dwarf then carried him inside and left him in a large room furnished richly. Ravana found he could grow back to his normal size. His confidence came back, and he clutched his mace tightly ready for whatever happened next.

A stalwart man came in. He was unarmed and had the kindest eyes Ravana had ever seen.

In his presence, Ravana calmed down. He felt peace in his heart. The man gestured to Ravana to sit.

The man smiled at the question he saw in Ravana's eyes. "I am Bali, son." He spoke.

Ravana was surprised and felt a little stupid. He had come to rescue Bali and found him to be ruling a rich land, and Ravana had to be rescued from the gatekeeper.

Bali laughed at the expression on Ravana's face. "Ravana, don't feel bad at losing to my gatekeeper, that was Vishnu in his dwarf avatar. One boon I received from Vishnu was that he would be my gatekeeper in this world. No one can win over the Lord of the world."

Ravana shrugged; he had gotten over his awe. "Come with me and I will make you again a king on Earth, King of any kingdom you choose." Urged Ravana.

Bali looked at him with pity and sorrow. "There is so much good in you Ravana, but all that is of no use. Your ego and pride blind your thoughts, leading you to a destructive path."

"Ravana, my time on Earth is over. The lord came to release me from that bond, not to punish me. Our lives are cyclic. I rule here, for now. Maybe in the next phase I will rule heaven as the new Indra. Happiness is doing your best in the circumstances." Advised Bali.

Ravana hated to receive advice. He got up in a huff and left the palace of Bali. He returned to Lanka and sulked over his failure, determined to do something that would shake the world.

Mahabali sighed. What a waste of potential, he thought.

Navaratri, the power of women

Navaratri is a nine-day celebration all over India of the victory of the Goddess over Mahishasur.

The Gujarat Navaratri celebration is world-famous, full of colour rhythms, swirling skirts and flashing eyes.

It is nine nights of fun and frolic in Gujarat, and it is great fun. I was lucky to be part of such celebrations for many years.

The Gujarat celebrations are well known.

The celebrations in the South of India are different, but equally colourful and fun.

There are different versions of the story. The popular one in the south is of the defeat of Mahishasur at the hands of the Goddess Durga.

Mahishasur was a powerful Asura and a great devotee of the creator Brahma.

Mahishasur, like many men, was power-mad, aggressive and had a poor opinion of women.

He, as was the practice then, undertook severe penance to get the favour of Brahma.

Something like what many of us in employment do, seek attention from the boss.

Brahma noticed his efforts and offered Mahishasur a boon.

Mahishasur sought a boon that any male or any animal should not defeat him.

He was confident no woman could ever overcome him.

It was a mistake many men indulge in, with disastrous consequences.

The Asura, blinded by his ego and a false belief in his strength, started a campaign of conquest and terror.

Indra and the devas were defeated and, as was their habit, cried in front of Brahma for giving the boon to the Asura that no male could defeat him.

A worried Brahma took them to Vishnu.

Vishnu decided that this required consultation with Shiva and all of them went to Mount Kailas.

They found Shiva and explained the problem to them.

Shiva smiled at them and said it is beyond all of us and only one person can help us.

He took them to Parvathi, his wife, and laid the problem before her.

"As usual, you men create the mess and we women have to clean it up," rasped Parvathi.

She called her lady friends and all the goddesses came and Parvathi assumed the form of Durga to battle with the Asura and his hordes.

It was a furious battle as the Asura kept changing shape and moving rapidly to escape. Durga found it difficult to battle alone.

All the goddesses then transferred their power to Durga and changed into statues.

This combined strength enabled Durga to win and destroy Mahishasur after a long battle and he was killed on Vijayadashmi day.

Dusshera or Navratri celebrates this; the power of women.

Mahishasur represents a lack of knowledge, a lack of civilisation and culture. These cannot be possible without the feminine force in our life.

In Hinduism, the Goddesses bless you with health, strength, wealth and knowledge. Without their blessing, you cannot achieve any of this.

It also denotes the strength of women. When they come together, nothing can stop them.

The other goddesses gave up their power and became statues to enable Durga to defeat the forces of darkness.

This sacrifice is celebrated and remembered by keeping the "Kollu".

During the nine days of Navaratri, there is a display of dolls on steps.

The number of steps traditionally would be in odd numbers.

The top steps will have the dolls of goddesses and the gods.

These dolls are traditionally handmade and of clay, but now you have wooden dolls and other materials are also used.

The bottom ones would depict life and have many themes like a city or rural life, a court scene, a Darbar or anything you like.

The women mostly set it up and they give expression to their artistic ideas in setting up the Kolu.

The women invite their friends and relatives to see the Kolu at their house and during evenings, the women in their finery go to each other's houses.

As children, we would also accompany our mothers, but our interest would be in the snacks served. The "chundal" or Sundal would be of different types on different days, mostly channa, chickpeas, etc. All spiced lightly with mustard seeds, ginger, coconut, etc.

The Dusshera at Mysore is a Royal Pageant famous the world over. The Kolus can be seen everywhere in this lovely city, including places of business.

Mysore has a large shop selling traditional dolls where you can spend hours admiring the creativity of the displays and the variety.

They range from small individual pieces to large sets, which depict various events like the Royal procession during Mysore Dusshera.

Navaratri is thus a celebration of womanhood and a reminder to men to not underestimate the power of a woman.

Panipuri and the Mahabharata

Panipuri is one of the most popular street foods in India. It is known by different names in different parts of the country.

I grew up in Mumbai and we call it the Panipuri.

The dish consists of crisp small puris; you punch an opening on the top and fill it with a bit of boiled potatoes, sweet chutney, and spicy chutney.

You pop it into your mouth, and when you bite into it, the various flavours fill your mouth.

The chutneys are watery, and the spicy one is virtually spiced water. So, the dish is a puri with water so we in Mumbai keep it simple and call it a Panipuri.

The Panipuri lends itself admirably to experimentation. Today, you have so many types and variations. There is even one where you fill up vodka and bite into it.

But the origins of the Panipuri are ancient, they knew it in ancient Magadha nearly 600 years BCE!

The original Panipuri in Magadha differed somewhat from the Panipuri as we know it today.

It was crisp puris filled with a mixture of vegetables, not potato, as it introduced the potato in India only about 600 years back.

The mythological origin of the Panipuri is the typical Indian tale of mothers-in-law and daughters-in-law.

The Pandavas were in hiding from the Kauravas and survived by disguising themselves as Brahmins. They subsisted on alms and had little.

It was then that Arjuna; the Pandava, won Draupadi at a swyamvar by proving to be the best archer in all of Aryavartha.

Draupadi is married to all the five Pandavas as commanded by their mother Kunti.

Their situation is precarious, the new daughter-in-law has come home to their poor hut, and the five Pandava brothers are enamoured with their beautiful bride.

Kunti, not too happy with this fascination, tests her new daughter-in-law.

She gives Draupadi a little flour, some leftover vegetables and asks her to make a dish that will satisfy the different tastes of all the five Pandava brothers.

So Draupadi invents Panipuri, hollow puffed puris in which you put vegetables of your choice, increase the sweetness or the spiciness by the use and change in the quantity of the different chutneys.

Draupadi had a best seller in hand. Kunti grudgingly agreed that her daughter-in-law was a fit bride for her sons.

So next time you bite into a Panipuri and let those heavenly flavours of sweet, sour, and spice fill your mouth, say thanks to Draupadi, a remarkable woman who has no equal.

If you think out of the box, a solution to the most difficult situations will be found.

Hanuman and Arjuna

Arjuna was in exile for a transgression of the agreement between the Pandavas about their common wife, Draupadi.

During this period, he wandered all over India and thus he reached Dhanushkodi in present day Tamil Nadu.

Arjuna prayed at the temple of Siva at Rameswaram, which was built by Sriram.

From there, Arjuna proceeded to nearby Dhanushkodi and gazed upon the two oceans which met there.

From Dhanushkodi, faint on the horizon, he could see Lanka. He also saw the remnants of the great bridge which Rama had built over the sea from Dhanushkodi to Lanka.

Arjuna sat and meditated on Sriram, but his ego was in the way. They celebrated Arjuna as the greatest Archer of his time, a warrior who had no equal.

Like all persons who excel, Arjuna also had supreme confidence in his ability. This confidence manifested itself as pride, and at such times, he needed a lesson in humility.

As Arjuna sat watching the ocean, he was sure he could easily have a made a bridge of arrows from Dhanushkodi to Lanka.

Sri Ram was also a great archer and warrior, the best of his times.

Arjuna, therefore, wondered aloud why did Sriram, the great archer, take the trouble to build a bridge with the help of the Vanaras, the monkeys. He could have easily built one with his arrows.

There was a small monkey on the beach sitting on a rock nearby. The monkey turned and laughed at Arjuna!

Arjuna, surprised and irritated, raised his eyebrows and asked the monkey, "What's so funny, you little vermin?"

The monkey shrugged and replied, "You are foolish to think a bridge of arrows could support mighty warriors like Sugreeva, Nila, Jambavan, or Angad. "

"In that age," continued the monkey, "we vanaras were a mighty tribe full of great warriors devoted to Lord Rama. No bridge of arrows could support the weight of that army."

Arjuna was not convinced and, mocking the little monkey, said, "Yes, I can see how big and strong you are".

The monkey curled its lips, showing sharp little teeth. "Yes, I am little, but can you make a bridge which will support my weight? "

Arjuna looked at him in surprise. "Don't you know who I am? I am Arjuna, the world's greatest archer,"

The monkey shrugged its tiny shoulders. "All men look alike to me and I have never heard of Arjuna. How does a human matter to me? Once Sriram left, you humans forgot about us. You ravaged the land, burnt the forests. "

Arjuna was now angry, his ego bruised. "I will build the bridge and it will bear your weight. If it does not, I will enter the fire," said Arjuna, now rash with anger.

The monkey agreed to the wager. Arjuna stepped near to the sea. He shot arrow after arrow and soon a shining, magnificent bridge was ready.

Arjuna proudly invited the monkey to step onto the bridge.

The monkey moved forward and was hesitant to step on the bridge. It put its tail on the bridge and the bridge collapsed!

The monkey turned around; its eyes fixed in an accusing glare on Arjun. "Are you trying to drown me?" It screamed at Arjuna.

A shocked Arjuna still held on to his confidence. He asked for another chance and the monkey agreed.

The bridge this time had arrows placed closer. Arjuna put all his skill into it. He was confident that it would hold this time.

The monkey moved forward and put one of its paws on the bridge, and it collapsed!

Arjuna was now humbled and devastated. He built a pyre for a fire.

There was a hail, and they saw a young ascetic walking towards them.

The young man wanted to know what was happening, and Arjuna explained the situation to him.

The ascetic laughed. "This is not the correct way to go about a wager. You need someone to judge. If you both will agree, I will be the judge and you can try again."

Arjuna was sure he would fail, but at the monkey's insistence, he agreed.

Arjuna shot his arrows and made the bridge again as strong as he could.

The monkey put a paw on the bridge; it held. Reluctantly and carefully, the monkey walked on it; the bridge held.

The monkey jumped up and down. The bridge remained steady.

The monkey was now scratching its head. It suddenly grew to an enormous size.

An amazed and awestruck Arjuna stood and gazed at the tremendous form of Hanuman in the form he took to leap the sea to Lanka.

Hanuman jumped up and down and hit the bridge with his mighty arms. The bridge did not even sway!

Arjuna was down on his knees, gaping at Hanuman in awe, but Hanuman was now smiling and he looked under the bridge.

There was the Sudarshan Chakra of Vishnu supporting the bridge underneath.

Hanuman walked off and prostrated himself in front of the young ascetic.

The ascetic lifted Hanuman and hugged him. "You remain as you ever were, my friend mischievous and bringing egos down."

Hanuman, now in his normal form, laughed. "Arjuna doubted you, my lord, and I wanted to have some fun with him. I would not have let him enter the fire."

As Arjuna watched this in amazement, the ascetic changed into Krishna, the avatar of Vishnu.

Krishna looked at Arjuna in silence for a while as Arjuna sat there in front of him with folded hands.

"Arjuna, the line between confidence and overconfidence is thin. Once you breach that line, your confidence becomes pride, your ego. This ego will cloud your thoughts and your judgment, leading to mistakes that can be fatal," said Krishna.

"Take this lesson to heart, my Arjun, and be thankful to Hanuman for teaching you this," said Krishna.

An embarrassed Arjuna got up and prostrated himself before Hanuman to seek his blessings. Hanuman laughed and blessed him and said, "the lord has come and shown me I too had pride in my strength. I will serve you in the great war that is imminent. I will be there on your flag and will lend my strength to your chariot."

Thus, these two great disciples of Vishnu were brought to a sense of their overconfidence and pride by Krishna.

In today's world, we see so many disasters caused by the ego and overconfidence of man and, sadly; the world pays for their mistakes.

Rama and the Rooster

How the rooster got its crown.

It devastated Ram when he came back from hunting the golden deer and found Sita missing

Ram was not aware of his divinity and reacted as any normal man would do.

Like all good husbands, he was attached to Sita and he could not bear finding her gone.

He cried and wailed; he blamed Lakshman for not staying back to look after her.

He could not think rationally, so great was his sorrow and despair. He lost heart and could not control his mind.

He first thought some wild animal might have attacked her, but there were no tracks around.

Life in the forest had been hard. Sita was a princess accustomed to the luxuries of life. Ram, in his despair, feared she might have been tired of the onerous forest life and left him to go back to her maternal home.

For Ram, the thought that Sita had grown tired of this life and gone back to her parents was unbearable.

This would besmirch his reputation, and once back in her own home, she would be reluctant to come back.

Sita's parents also would not let her come back to a hard life in the forest. Sita was beloved by her parents and her siblings.

In Ayodhya too, Sita was a favourite of everyone. Ram could not bear the thought of going back to Ayodhya and facing his family without her.

The idea took hold of him, and nothing that Lakshman said would console him. He could not believe anyone could have come and kidnapped her.

He was convinced he had annoyed her and tired of the hard life of the forest. Sita had left him and gone home.

As Ram sat in sorrow, a rooster strutted into view. The rooster cocked his head and looked at the strange sight of a stalwart human crying.

The rooster walked up to Lakshman and politely made a dignified inquiry about the matter.

Lakshman would normally have been brusque and impatient of such an inquiry. After all, a rooster was an insignificant being in the forest.

But so shaken was Lakshman that he told the entire story to the Rooster.

The rooster strutted up to Ram and offered his greetings. He sat and listened to Rams' worries.

The rooster after listening to Ram told him he, Ram, was wrong. The rooster had seen a rakshasa carrying off a crying lady in a flying chariot.

The rooster called his flock to him and they also confirmed that they had also seen a crying lady struggling and being carried away by a rakshasa in a flying chariot.

The Rooster patiently explained what he had seen. Other small animals were called by the rooster to support his story.

He convinced Rama that Sita had been abducted. He encouraged Rama to find and save her.

A rejuvenated Ram stood up, strong, fiercely determined to save his wife.

What Lakshman could not do; the small rooster had done.

Ram smiled affectionately at the rooster and offered him a crown of gold to wear.

The Rooster would have none of it.

It replied, "oh lord now only some men chase me to hunt, kill and eat me, and that too if they don't get the bigger game."

"If I have a crown of Gold, all men will hunt me in their greed for the Gold. I would much rather prefer a crown of flesh."

Smiling, Ram gave the rooster a coloured magnificent crown of flesh. And that's why all roosters have a crown over their heads, unlike the hens.

So, the lord taught us two lessons in this simple story.

Whoever you are, you can still make a difference.

Even Lord Ram needs his wife, so be good to the lady in your life.

Shadows and Sorcery

We know the Mahabharata has many local legends added with local cultural flavours in it.

Kerala, God's own country, as we call it, is in the southern part of India, it is a beautiful land with swaying coconut palms, sea-washed beaches, soaring mountains, verdant forests, and lush paddy fields, and stories of sorcery and magic.

So, inevitably, the stories from Kerala would have a flavour quite unlike what you would find in the Gangetic plains.

There is a song in Kerala which used to be sung by wandering minstrels. The song tells of Duryodhana employing a sorcerer to kill the Pandavas and how they were saved by Krishna.

People believe that singing these songs protects the house and its residents from the evil eye and black magic.

Mantra Vadis, or Mantrikans as sorcerers are called, were common in Kerala, people could be hire them to do whatever they wished.

Later, the story in this song became a Kathakali drama about a century ago. It was a popular story and often staged during the night-long performances at the temples.

The story is like this.

Duryodhana was worried. The Pandavas were in exile in the forest, but they were getting stronger, gathering support. Arjuna was gathering new and more powerful Astras, and the day of reckoning would come soon.

Shakuni, Duryodhana's maternal uncle, sly and scheming, watched as Duryodhana paced up and down.

They were in the Southern part of their empire near the tall Malaya mountains, the southern parts of the western ghats.

"Duryodhana, I was in one of the nearby villages where the mountain dwellers live and they told me about a powerful sorcerer who lives deep inside the forest. He is a master of sorcery; they say he can control the darkness and make shadows do his will. Let us consult with him," advised Shakuni.

Duryodhana hesitated. He was a peerless warrior who liked to meet his enemies head-on. But jealousy, greed, and ambition had taken hold inside him.

He was alone with Shakuni, whose mind was twisted and dark. There was no Karna to protest, no Ashwatthama to decry such evil. Bhishma, Vidur, Vikarna, and all the others who would have opposed such a dark deed were absent.

There was only the brawny but brainless Dushasna for company, and he was always in agreement with anything that would harm the Pandavas.

Shakuni saw the opportunity to remove the Pandavas and tarnish the reputation of the Kauravas forever. He would finally have his revenge on the Kurus for what they had done to his kingdom and his sister. Bhishma would be heartbroken, devastated.

It would be sweet revenge for Shakuni, who still was seething with anger when he thought about his sister being forced to marry a blind fool like Dhritarashtra.

Shakuni loved his nephews, but his thirst for revenge was stronger, like it was in all people from Gandhar. They would act ruthlessly and without humanity and seek revenge. It was in their blood and it continues till today.

Shakuni set to work on Duryodhana, reminding him of all the insults he had faced, the perceived injustice of denying Duryodhana the throne.

Duryodhana, blinded by rage, called a messenger to summon the sorcerer to his presence.

The messenger came back; the sorcerer was not in his home; he was on the mountain top doing penance and would be back home in two days. He would present himself in front of Duryodhana on the fourth day from today. This was the reply from the sorcerer's wife.

The Sorcerer Malayan came back refreshed, his magic restored at full strength because of his penance. Happily, he entered his small house deep in the forest.

His wife, Malayati, met him, her face gloomy and distraught. Malayan was worried. Had he committed a wrong, were his in-laws well, did his parents say something nasty to her or his biggest fear, did she take a lover when he was away?

Every husband is like that, always in doubt about himself and in fear of his wife. Be it a King or a great sorcerer.

But Malayati put those fears to rest. "There has been a summons from Prince Duryodhana, which you cannot refuse. We are poor people. God only knows how this will end. Nothing good comes from standing before these great men. It is like standing behind a donkey. Both will kick and hurt you for no reason." Malayati said sadly.

The omens were not good, and it was with some unease that Malayan prepared for his journey the next day.

Malayati told him to go meet Kunti and the Pandavas who were living nearby in the forest while coming back and tell them about the meeting with Duryodhana. Malayati was a devotee of Krishna and a passionate supporter of the Pandavas. She admired Kunti, the mother of the Pandavas.

Duryodhana was having second thoughts about calling for a sorcerer who lived hidden in the woods. Why would he do that? Duryodhana did not understand that Malayan did it to avoid people using him for evil acts. Powerful people who did not want to dirty their hands always hired people like Malayan, a forest dweller, for such acts.

Malayan was a gentle soul, like most tribals and those who live close to nature.

He used his powers for good, to heal people, find lost valuables and sometimes catch a thief. He accepted whatever the people gave him. He lived quietly and did this only for the tribals like him, avoiding cities and powerful people.

Duryodhana called his friend Trigarthan, a great warrior who had accompanied him. He asked him to guard the gates of the royal house and not allow Malayan to enter. This would help Duryodhana understand whether Malayan was as powerful as people said he was.

Malayan came to the palace early the next day and found Trigarthan astride an enormous elephant blocking his way along with a powerful force of armed men

With the power of his sorcery, Malayan created a wall of fire that moved towards the people blocking his path. The soldiers and the elephant fled, carrying Trigarthan away, and Malayan reluctantly entered the palace.

Duryodhana was convinced this man could do what many others could not do. He would remove the Pandavas from his path.

Malayan stood humbly with hands folded, before Shakuni and Duryodhana.

"It is said that you can capture a person's shadow and kill him by stabbing the shadow. Is this true?". Asked Shakuni. Duryodhana kept quiet and watched.

Malayan was reluctant, but he could not lie. He nodded, "Yes, I can, my lord, but it takes too much of my powers and it is prohibited."

"You will capture the shadows of the Pandavas and kill them, or else we will kill your wife and son. Even now your house is surrounded by my men, even if you escape from here unless we give the word, they will slaughter your family."

"If you do this, we will give you half the kingdom. You will be a king and your family safe. If you don't listen to us, we will kill you now." Said Shakuni.

Dushasna drew his sword and placed it on Malayan's neck.

Malayan looked into the cruel eyes of these great men and knew the loss of hope. He had no choice. If he did this cruel horrifying act, he would lose all his powers and no penance would restore it. He would go mad with guilt.

He accepted his fate to save his wife and child.

He sat down on the floor and invoked the dark forces; his powers forced them out of the nether world.

The daylight disappeared, and the hall was dark, filled by growling evil spirits muttering their anger at this call.

The orders they received to capture and bring the shadows of the Pandavas stopped them. The spirits became silent. "This is an evil thing you ask us Malayan, think well before you insist, the sin will be yours alone." said the spirits.

"I am forced by the prince here and have no choice," replied Malayan.

"We will bring the shadows of the Pandavas, but we will not kill them. The sin of killing them will be yours, Malayan," said the spirits.

They placed a large mirror in front of the sorcerer, the shadows of the Pandavas appeared one by one. But Malayan saw that there was an additional shadow that appeared on its own, the shadow of Krishna.

The shadow of Krishna watched and then vanished. Malayan was now terrified.

He hesitated and turned to Duryodhana and pleaded, "Lord, please reconsider. The Pandavas are under Lord Krishna's protection. Nothing good will come from such an evil act."

Duryodhana was beyond reason now. His goal seemed very near. "Do your job, sorcerer, leave the repercussions to me or face the death now," he replied.

The sword of Dushasna was on his neck. There was no choice for Malayan.

He began chanting the incantations. He drew the sacrificial knife and cut off the finger of one servant there, who screamed in agony.

The cut finger and the blood dripping from the servant he offered to the spirits.

The room grew darker still; the air grew heavy, the angry growls of the reluctant spirits grew, and the sacrificial knife glowed with its evil power.

Malayan took the knife and stabbed the shadow of Yudhishtra. There was a cry that rang faintly in the room, and they could see the blood flow from the wound in the shadow.

Yudhishtra fell.

Now beyond caring and in the grip of the evil act, Malayan quickly stabbed the other Pandavas.

The great Bhima fell without a sound, Arjuna the archer lay limp and lifeless and the twins had no breath.

The shadows in the mirror vanished and Malayan stood aghast at what he had done.

There was silence in the hall. Slowly, the darkness lifted, and Duryodhana shouted with joy.

If Malayan expected thanks or the promised half of the kingdom, he was in for a rude shock.

Shakuni turned to Malayan, "Here, take these five coins. That is all that these Pandavas are worth. Speak nothing of what has happened here if you value your life."

Malayan turned. There was a glimmer of hope in his eyes. "What about half the kingdom you promised me" he asked.

The evil men in the hall roared with laughter. "Go now before I lose my temper and kill you," said Duryodhana. Malayan was driven away from the palace.

Malayan stepped out empty-handed. He left the five coins inside the palace. He would take no payment for this evil act.

A worried and unhappy Malayan reached home. He did not go to see Kunti. Malayati was feeding their son, the baby was suckling at her breast.

She looked at Malayan and knew he had done a terrible act. He had promised her he would never use his powers to kill.

She forced him to tell her all that had happened and when she heard he had killed the Pandavas; she cried out in anger.

Malayati was mad with rage. "You evil man, you have killed five children of a widowed mother. How will Kunti survive this? You do not deserve any happiness; you too should know the agony of losing a child." She screamed at him.

In a paroxysm of rage, she pulled the baby from her breast, and with inhuman strength, held the baby by his legs and tore the child apart.

Malayan looked at the torn body of his beloved son. His mind snapped, he shivered in agony, his heart burst with grief and he fell dead beside the mutilated body of his son.

Malayati, mad with grief and anger, ran with her bloody hands to the hut of the Pandavas and fell at the feet of a sorrowing Kunti.

Kunti sat by the bodies of her slain, stalwart sons. Her world had come crashing down.

She listened to the pleadings of Malayati and within her broken heart, Kunti found strength and compassion. She held the sobbing Malayati to her, both of them united in their grief.

Such is this world, men fight and stride about with their egos, kill and maim. Women suffer and cry.

Krishna was calm and had a smile on his face when the women saw him.

The women got up in anger and glared at him. How could he be so calm in the face of such tragedy?

He looked at them and said gently, "Do you have so little faith in me? Malayati, you have committed the greater sin. They forced your husband into what he did. No blame attaches to him. He did not get half the kingdom as promised and he also left the five coins given to him. He is blameless."

Krishna looked at Malayati in great sorrow. "How could you do this? How could you tear your child from your breast and kill that innocent son of yours? Yours is the heinous act Malayati, not your husband's."

"Any act which is done without thought in anger or pique will lead to adharma. You Malayati have done such an act which is as heinous as that done by the Kauravas. No, it is eviler. The Kauravas acted against their enemies. You killed your child, whom you should have protected. You are attached to my aunt Kunti. Look how she supports and protects her children." Krishna continued to address Malayati, who was now in despair.

"Krishna, enough of this advice. You have promised to protect my children. You have broken it," said Kunti.

Krishna turned to her, "Aunt, you know I always keep my promises". Krishna used his divine powers and restored the Pandavas to life.

Malayati was broken, and in despair, Krishna took pity on her. She was also his devotee. He sighed. It was always like this. Men and women acted in haste and he had to step in. Why, even the Devas, celestial gods did the same.

He lifted Malayati, "Go child, back to your house. I have restored your husband and child. Let this be a lesson for you. Your actions have tainted you; you will not get salvation and not be able to be with your husband and child. They will leave you. Only when you are united with them will you get salvation."

Malayati ran back and found her husband and child restored to life. But life had changed for them. Malayati's actions had caused a wound that would never heal.

The father took his son and vanished deep into the forests, away from the world of men and its sorrows.

Malayati ran after them, but they eluded her. Even today, if you walk among the forests of Wayanad and listen to the wind, you can hear Malayati wailing and calling out to her son.

Swaminatha and Om, the primordial sound

Om is the primordial sound in Hinduism. It has a sophisticated, complex meaning and there have been entire books written about it. It is also called the Pranava Mantra.

To put it simply, Om is Atman, the soul, our breath, our consciousness. But the word soul here has different meanings than the straitjacket sense of soul in western culture.

It denotes the Atman, the soul in us, it also denotes the Brahman, the supreme consciousness. The soul and everything else are within the Brahman, but the Brahman is also within us.

Thus, simply put, we can say that we are the universe, and the universe is us.

Yes, a rather confusing idea, but all philosophy is complex and confusing until you get the core idea.

But we are here to know why Karthikeyan or Murugan, the God of war came to be called Swaminatha.

Karthikeyan, the son of Shiva and Parvathi, was an intelligent child befitting his illustrious parents. His knowledge was precocious.

His parents wanted the best of education for him, as all Indian parents do for their children.

So, they sent him to Brahma, the creator. The lessons from Brahma did not satisfy Karthikeyan. He was constantly asking Brahma questions. One day, Karthikeyan asked the meaning of the word Om.

Now even Brahma did not know the answer and expressed his inability to explain the meaning of Om

A disappointed Karthikeyan immediately started back and reached Kailasa, the abode of Shiva and Parvathi.

Shiva, as befitting his nature, was calm at the return of his son without completing his education.

Parvathi was concerned and agitated at the return. Both parents sat with the child to understand his premature return.

"Why have you returned my son before completing your education?" asked Shiva.

"I wanted to know the meaning of Om and Brahma could not explain it to me," replied Karthikeyan.

Shiva smiled at that. "Child, even I do not know the complete meaning of the Pranava mantra, Brahma is the creator, his knowledge is vast. Please go back and complete your education."

Karthikeyan looked at Shiva in the eye and told him, "I know the meaning of the Pranava Mantra. "

Shiva was smiling at his precocious son. "Then explain the meaning to me, Karthikeyan," said Shiva.

"I will if you accept me as your Guru and seat me higher than you," said Karthikeyan.

An amused Shiva lifted his small son and put him on his shoulder. Thus, Karthikeyan was sitting in an elevated position as compared to Shiva.

Sitting on Shiva's shoulder, Karthikeyan whispered the meaning of the mantra to an amazed Shiva.

A proud mother, Parvathi, sat and watched with happiness her son teaching her husband, who was himself a renowned teacher.

In her happiness and pride in her son, Parvathi called him Swami (Guru) natha (her husband). Which means Guru of my husband.

Thus, Karthikeyan gained his name Swaminatha or Swaminathan by teaching his father Shiva himself.

Today, we cannot keep up with the quick advances that take place in technology. Thus, we may need to learn from someone much younger. We should accept this learning from someone younger but more knowledgeable with the grace that Shiva showed in learning from his son.

The Emperor and the Courtesan

As per ancient Indian stories, everyone has a dharma. Be it a king, a common citizen, animals, trees, everything has a dharma to which one has to be true.

If we are true to your dharma, we can use it as a mantra to get nature to do your will. This is called an "act of truth".

Our stories are full of such acts of truth. An example is Sita sitting on the fire and saying, "if I am chaste, let not the fire harm me." The fire accepts her truth and does not harm her, thus confirming her truth. This is Sita's act of truth.

In ancient Indian tales, there is a story of Bindumati, the courtesan and her act of truth

She lived in Patliputra, that great city, the capital of Emperor Asoka. She was a common courtesan well past her prime, irreverent, and filled with the joy of life.

Emperor Asoka was tired of war. He now followed the teachings of Buddha and sent learned men around the world to propagate the teachings of the master. His court was full of learned men, great pundits, philosophers and holy men.

One day the Ganges rose. The city watched in fear as the floodwaters swirled and threatened the city itself.

The emperor and the people gathered and watched the mighty river swell. Soon the river was lapping at the walls of the city. The people in this section were poor and rushed to the emperor and sought his help.

The emperor wrung his hands and cried, "is there no one here who can stop the river, no one who can do an act of truth and turn the river away?"

The holy men, the pundits, the wise and the learned, mumbled but kept quiet.

Out of the crowd below walked out a lady in simple clothes. She stood before the waters of the mighty Ganges. She raised her hand and spoke her truth. The river waters subsided and turned away from the city!

The emperor had the lady brought before him and was astonished to see Bindumati, the old prostitute of Patliputra.

The old courtesan grinned at him, showing her betel nut reddened teeth.

"Oh, mighty King, do you remember me?" she asked.

The emperor blushed. Almost every man in the city knew Bindumati.

"How did you stop the river, Bindu? What act of truth could you speak?" asked a bewildered emperor.

"My truth is I accept all men as equal, whether rich or poor, handsome or ugly, young or old. I treat them equally with no discrimination or differentiation, if they pay my price, as that is my dharma, oh King," said Bindumati.

"That is my truth, oh lord, as a courtesan and the river accepted it." Said Bindumati.

The King and the people there realised that the truth is the same for everyone. One does one's job or dharma without bias. They also realised anyone can perform an act of truth, be they high born, low born, educated, rich, poor or unlearned. The truth does not differentiate.

The emperor returned to the palace as a wiser man. And Bindumati, she returned home. What she had done was only her dharma, and dharma is its own reward, so she got nothing more from Asoka.

The Golden Mongoose

The war was over; corpses had piled up on the battlefield, mangled, cut, shredded, burnt. They lay there oozing blood and gore.

Their sightless eyes seemed to mock him as Yudhishtra, the victor, looked at the battlefield of Kurukshetra.

They had won the victory at an unbearable cost. The Pandavas had lost all their children. They had killed Karna, their own eldest brother. They had killed their grand sire, Bhishma.

Their cousins, the Kauravas, met a brutal death at the hands of the Pandavas, especially Bhima.

Yudhishtra was now the Emperor of the Kurus, a hollow title it seemed to him hearing the wails of the women.

The women huddled together. Among them, there was no animosity. For them, the war was the enemy. They wailed for their lovers; they wailed for husbands lost, fathers killed, and above all, they wailed for their children killed in the prime of life.

Yudhishtra could bear it no longer. He fled to the palace, the screams and wails following him.

The days passed and nature asserted itself. The war was a memory now, a bitter one, but life moved on, and ruling a vast empire had its troubles.

Yudhishtra had adjusted and so had his brothers.

The kingdom was peaceful, prosperous now, and the Pandavas wanted the memory of the brutal war to end.

They consulted the wise men of the land who advised them to conduct a grand yagna, a sacrifice where all who come would be given gifts from the Treasury.

Wise men are always the same. They advise the rulers to give to the public gifts to assuage the guilt, make the people forget their miseries. Just like they do before the elections now. The rulers call it a sacrifice and give gifts to the people. But the gifts come from the treasury and the Treasury is the public money. The people sacrifice and the rulers gain credit.

So, the Pandavas organized the grandest yagna of all times. They loaded the people with gifts. The Brahmins received cows and grants. They gave the warriors gold and land. Common people got food, clothes, money.

Everyone who came was given something, and the treasury emptied. There were special pujas, entertainment every night, and there was a large dining area where everyone ate together of the choicest of food.

The crowds gathered and hailed the Yudhishtra and the Pandavas after every meal. They called this the greatest sacrifice ever done.

The Pandavas basked in this praise and even Yudhishtra, that upright, cerebral, and balanced man was carried away.

One day, as Yudhishtra, and the Pandavas sat puffed up, listening to the people singing their praises, there was a disturbance in the crowd.

Out of the crowd darted a mongoose, that small creature which fights the most venomous snakes with courage and confidence

But this was a strange mongoose. One side of the mongoose was gold, pure, lustrous, shining gold.

It looked at the crowd; it cocked its head and stared at Yudhishtra and the Pandavas. Its sharp eyes seemed to see everything and everyone in that glance.

Now a mongoose is a shy creature that avoids all crowds and this one was a half golden one. The crowd hushed their songs of praise and watched.

The mongoose darted to some fallen scraps of food but strangely did not eat it.

It rolled on the scraps of food and then looked at its own body. There was no change. It ran to other portions of the spilled food and rolled on them and again looked at its body.

The mongoose did this in many places where the food had fallen. The mongoose finally stopped its antics and looked at the crowd with disdain.

It looked at Yudhishtra and caught his eye and shook its head and said sadly, "no this is not the greatest sacrifice; it is not even an ordinary sacrifice."

The Pandavas and the crowd were amazed. A talking mongoose, what a wonder!

Bhima started forward in anger, he always was the angry man who hit first and thought about it later. Yudhishtra stopped him.

"Oh mongoose, you seem to be a divine and evolved soul. Please explain to us why you said this is not a sacrifice?" Said Yudhishtra.

The mongoose smiled and said, "oh king and all of you gathered here. Listen to my story."

This was the tale of the Golden Mongoose.

In a little unnamed village south of here lived a poor brahmin with his wife, his son, and his daughter-in-law.

His name is of no importance. He was neither a King nor a wise scholar. He was just an ordinary common man.

I lived in a little nest near their house and watched them and their life.

The brahmin and his son struggled to cultivate what little piece of land they had. They did small pujas and taught the village children the Vedas and Dharma. Somehow, they ate and stayed alive. The villagers were also poor, and they were far, far away from the capital of the empire.

They were unimportant people in a nondescript village like thousands of other villages.

No one from the King came with any help. The officer from the nearby town came once a year to collect the taxes. In times of trouble, he never came nor offered help.

This was how it had been for generations. While Empires were being built and destroyed, when warriors waged war and havoc, wise men debated on religion and philosophy, the little village remained unchanged.

Now it so happened that famine came to the land. There were no rains, and the land lay parched. Hunger and death roamed the land, walking hand in hand.

The villagers starved. There was no help from the King, he had already collected taxes for that year.

Those who could go, left, searching for food and a better life. The village was like a ghost village.

The brahmin and his family barely survived. It had been nearly a week now that they were subsisting on boiled water with a few grasses in it.

After a lot of foraging, the poor Brahmin had got a fistful of raw rice. The women in the house pounded it and boiled it along with the husk. They also found a little salt in the house. The rice gruel was bubbling in the fire and the family eagerly looked forward to eating this poor fare, which to them was life and survival itself.

The women had removed the gruel, put the salt in and carefully divided it into four equal parts.

They had just said their prayers before eating the gruel when there was a hesitant knock on the door.

They had nothing anyone could steal, so they opened the door with no fear.

An emaciated-looking ascetic stood there asking for food.

Now dharma says you cannot turn a hungry man from your door, you share with him.

The Brahmin, a teacher of Dharma, believed in it wholeheartedly. How could he turn away from a hungry man?

The brahmin invited the ascetic in and offered the ascetic his portion of the gruel.

As the family watched, the ascetic finished the gruel in one large gulp. The ascetic was still hungry and asked for some more. The Brahmin's wife offered her portion, but the Brahmin protested "you need to have your portion or you will not survive the night" he told her.

The wife would have none of it. She told the Brahmin, "As you wife, I am your ardhangani and not separate from you. What you have done as dharma has no meaning if I don't share in it.".

The Brahmin was silent. In Indian culture, the husband and wife are one entity for that life, the wife is one half, the ardhangani of the single entity. The better half, as we would say in English. A man was incomplete without his wife and his actions alone have no merit.

The ascetic watched this in silence and eagerly accepted the wife's portion when it was given. He slurped it up quickly and asked for more.

The poor Brahmin was aghast. What could he do? He gathered his courage and will to break dharma and refuse any more food to the ascetic.

The Brahmin's son then offered his portion. The son told his father, "I am your only son, and it is my duty to help you do your duty and meet your obligation."

The Brahmin watched silently as the ascetic finished the portion belonging to the son.

The ascetic put the vessel down and asked for more. The daughter-in-law stepped forward. She was ardhangani to the son and had to support him.

As the ascetic finished the last portion, the Brahmin and his family watched. He was finally satisfied. He thanked and blessed the family and stepped out on his way.

The Brahmin and his family spent the whole day searching for something to eat but could find nothing.

It was night, and the family lay together, hands clasped, shivering with hunger. I watched from a hole in the wall of their hut.

I knew they would not survive the night. As dawn came peeping inside the Brahmin and his family prepared to shrug off this life.

There was then a blinding light, and there stood Lord Indra, the king of gods. He had been the ascetic, and he had come to reward the family for their sacrifice.

The Brahmin wanted nothing for himself as that would negate his sacrifice, but prayed that Indra would take pity on the parched land and give it rain.

Indra agreed, and thunder rumbled, and lightning flashed in the air. The rain came down in torrents and the parched land soaked it up. Indra left, blessing the family. The family rushed out to enjoy the rain.

I saw that there was some gruel fallen on the ground and rushed to have it. I slipped on the wet ground and rolled in the gruel. Wherever the gruel touched me, I turned Golden. But there was only enough to turn half my body Golden.

Since then, I have gone to all the places where a yagna or sacrifice was being made, hoping to turn my other half also Golden.

I heard about this yagna. People said you were doing the greatest of all sacrifices. I came here with high hopes but leave disappointed.

All I found was another king wasting the resources of the Kingdom to enhance his name.

Oh, King, your yagna does not meet even a small part of the great sacrifice I had witnessed.

The mongoose then vanished in a flash.

Yudhishtra was stunned, as were all the people gathered there. The yagna had ended.

Yudhishtra was dharma incarnate, he was the son of Yama, the God of death and dharma.

He understood the message of the mongoose. A sacrifice is a sacrifice only if it is given from one's resources. A sacrifice is where one gives with no motive in the spirit of giving. Otherwise, it is only a trade.

The Golden Snake

We grew up listening to or reading fairy tales. Most of what we read were western fairy tales.

I would often find some similarities between stories from different lands and Indian tales. It was only much later that I learnt many of these tales had originated in India as per many scholars.

Most of us know the story of the Goose that laid golden eggs. We even had a poem in school where it was a hen that laid the golden eggs.

But there is an old story I heard long ago from a villager in Gujarat which is similar and yet different. Now, which is the original one I don't know.

There are still a lot of studies and debates on the origins, but what has that to do with us? Let us just enjoy the tale.

There was once a farmer who was hardworking. He had sufficient land on which he grew crops to maintain his family.

They were a small family, the farmer, his wife and his son.

The farmer worked in the field but would not allow his son to work in the fields. The father wanted his son to become a learned and wise man. So, he sent him to the school in the city.

One day, the farmer went early to the fields and saw a giant golden snake slither out of the large tree in the centre of the field.

The farmer realised that this was one of the guardians of nature and left it alone. He returned home that night and told his wife about it.

The wife told him he should be grateful to the snake for protecting the land and thank the snake.

So, the next morning, the farmer took some milk and left it near the tree. When he returned, he found the milk gone and, in its place, a small gold nugget.

This became a regular practice; the farmer would leave an offering of food for the snake and would get a nugget of gold. He would sell the gold in the nearby town.

The farmer became well off but was careful to show no overt signs of his newfound prosperity.

In due time, the son came home after completing his studies. He had a lot of knowledge of the world. He could regale you about what they did in the land of the Nagas, how they lived in the Dravidian lands.

He could argue for hours with other learned people on dharma and Karma. But he did not know the land. He did not know what crops to sow, when to sow, or even tell the time by looking at the shadows of the trees.

He had a lot of learning which would not be of any use in taking care of the land or leading a practical life.

The worried farmer decided to consult his relatives and friends in the nearby town. He now had capital and could set up his son in some trade.

He called his son and told him about the giant golden snake and how the snake gave him a gold nugget for the food offered.

He told his son to take the food and leave it for the snake daily till he, the farmer, returned.

The son did so on the first day, not believing what his father had said. But, lo, in the evening the food was gone and there was a small gold nugget in its place.

The son took the food the next day and hoped to see the snake. He hid and saw the giant golden snake come out of the hole in the tree. It had a gold nugget in its mouth. He watched as the snake dropped the nugget and finished the food.

The son sat up in the night thinking, what a fool my father is taking food every day to a snake. There must be a hoard of the gold nuggets under that tree.

My father believes in all this old stuff. It is better to kill the snake, cut the tree and remove all the nuggets at once, thought the son.

The next day, he took the food to the snake and hid in the bushes. He had a heavy cudgel in his hand. As the snake bent its head to have the food, the son leapt out and hit it with his cudgel.

But the snakes are always alert and the Golden Snake moved its head away just in time and the blow fell on its body. It survived the blow.

The pain of the blow made the snake angry and, in a flash, it struck the son with its poison fangs.

The son fell dead, and the bruised snake slithered away.

The farmer came back in the evening and did not find his son at home. His wife told him that the boy had not returned since he went to the fields in the morning.

A worried father rushed to the field and found his dead son and the cudgel there. He knew then that his son's greed had got the better of him. He took the body away and cremated it in the night.

The next day, he went to the field with an offering of food and placed it before the tree. He waited and soon the snake came out.

The farmer folded his hands and said "Oh golden one my son, in his greed, did a foul deed. Forgive him and us. I have brought my offering. Please accept it and bless us as before."

The snake looked at him sadly and said, "you are equally greedy; you have lost your only son to me and still you come immediately and seek to offer me food so that you will continue to get your gold."

"I no longer trust you and I will leave this place; man's greed will be his downfall." Said the snake, slithering away.

The snake left, and the farmer cut down the tree, hoping to find a hoard of gold. He found nothing.

Without the tree and the snake, the fields dried up and rodents ate the crops and slowly the land lost its fertility.

The story tells us not only about greed but also about the balance in nature and the effect of disturbing that balance.

The Importance of a Guru

We celebrate Guru Purnima in India and Nepal. More than a religious festival, it is a cultural or traditional occasion.

It goes beyond religion in the sense that I wished a happy Guru Purnima to one of my schoolteachers who is a follower of Islam. He accepted my wishes and blessed me. This is a typical Indian practice that is followed irrespective of the faith one follows.

It is a celebration of those who share their wisdom, knowledge, and experience with us. Those who light up the path ahead for us.

Guru Purnima is not teacher's day; teacher's day celebrates Dr. S. Radhakrishnan's birthday. He was a philosopher and President of India.

Guru Purnima is considered the birthday of Veda Vyasa, the great guru who collected, edited, and gave the Vedas to the world.

A Guru is someone who is more connected to your spiritual well-being. You get knowledge from a teacher; you get wisdom along with knowledge from a guru.

This wisdom lets you know when and where to use your knowledge.

An ancient Indian tale highlights this.

There were once four friends in a village. Three of them were brilliant, while the fourth was a normal person, like most of us.

They all started their studies, and the three gained expert knowledge from their teachers.

The fourth one found a guru from whom he got wisdom.

After their education was over, the four friends met together and started back home.

The three bright students were full of their knowledge. They took every opportunity to show off and looked down at their ordinary friend.

They were crossing a thick forest, and the three were arguing who was the most learned when they came across the bones of an animal.

They stopped. This was an excellent opportunity to test and show off their knowledge.

The first one assembled the bones of the animal.

The second gave it flesh and blood.

The third proposed to give it life.

The fourth friend said "stop, don't give it life that is a lion and it will kill all of us."

The three friends laughed at their talentless friend. Even though he begged and pleaded with them, they would not listen to him.

They were adamant that they would use their knowledge.

The fourth friend scrambled up a tree quickly as the fourth chanted the required mantras to bring the animal back to life.

The lion opened its eyes and glared at the three friends who were congratulating each other.

There was a roar, screams, and knowledge was dead. The three friends died under the paws of the lion they had brought to life.

As they died, the lion also returned to its original form of a dried pile of bones.

The fourth friend came down and gazed sadly at his dead friends. "Alas, if they had gained wisdom along with knowledge, this would not have happened," he thought.

On Guru Poornima, may all of us be blessed with a Guru who gives us true wisdom.

My pranam to all the Gurus who have enriched me all these years.

The lamps of Diwali

During Diwali, we celebrate one day as Naraka Chaturdashi. Lamps are lit, coloured lights put up and people celebrate the death of Narakasura.

But who was this Narakasura and why is his death a cause for celebration?

Bhumi Devi, the Earth goddess, was being harassed by Hiranyaksha, who kidnapped her.

Vishnu, in his Varaha avatar, killed Hiranyaksha and rescued the Earth.

The Earth and Vishnu, as Varaha had a son who was called Naraka. The Mother sought a long life for her son. Vishnu gave Naraka the boon of power, a long life and that he would not be killed by any male. In some legends, it is said they gave him the boon that he could only be killed by the one who gave birth to him.

Naraka was a pious child, and his mother was proud of him. He grew up to be a powerful warrior, unmatched in strength and skill.

He conquered the lands around him and set up the fabled kingdom of Pragjyotisha after defeating the Danavas. This kingdom in the land known as Kamarupa (present-day Assam) was famed as a rich and fabled kingdom.

His power and his fame grew, and he married the beautiful princess Maya of Vidarbha.

Naraka became friends with Bana, the powerful son of Mahabali, the fabled king of Kerala.

Bana was thousand-armed, and a terror for the devas. He was called Banasura for his dark deeds.

You are known by the company you keep. Creating fear makes many feel powerful and feeds their ego. That is why it is said that power corrupts.

In Bana's company, Naraka became Narakasura.

He began harassing the devas; he lusted after women and did evil deeds.

It is said that he once desired Devi Khamkhaya.

He proposed to her, and she playfully told him that if he could build a staircase in one night to the top of the hill where her temple was located, she would marry him.

Naraka started building the staircase, and they soon saw that he would succeed. The Devi, who did not want to marry him, caught a cock and forced it to crow to indicate dawn.

Naraka stopped his work and only realised much later that they had tricked him.

He gave in fully to the dark side of him then and committed atrocities on the people and Devas. None could stop him.

He kidnapped women; he killed pious men, disturbed the sages in their meditation and made Indra flee from Swarga.

He was so drunk with power that he stole the earrings of Aditi, the mother goddess.

The Gods begged Vishnu for help.

Vishnu had taken the Krishna avatar. Naraka had lived for a long time and it was time to end his reign of terror.

Bhumidevi, the earth goddess, had taken the avatar of Satyabhama, the consort of Krishna.

Aditi, the mother, came and cried to Satyabhama about the atrocities of Naraka.

Satyabhama was furious and exhorted Krishna to end the reign of terror by Naraka.

Krishna promised to do so if Satyabhama helped him.

Satyabhama drove Krishna's chariot, and the battle began. Krishna destroyed the armies of Naraka but could not prevail over Naraka.

Krishna killed Mura, the fabled general of Naraka, and, hence, Krishna is also called Murari.

But Krishna could not kill Naraka, and neither could Naraka prevail over Krishna.

Krishna knew his mother, Bhumidevi, could only kill Naraka.

Satyabhama was Bhumidevi's avatar.

But how could a mother kill her son? Krishna took the next arrow from Naraka and pretended to faint and fall.

Satyabhama became mad with grief and anger at seeing Krishna's fall. She took up Krishna's Sudarshana Chakra and beheaded Naraka.

At the touch of the divine weapon and his mother, the evil in Naraka fled, the darkness in him gave way to light.

As a boon, he asked Satyabhama that his death should be celebrated by lighting lamps, signifying the dispersion of darkness by the light of knowledge.

Krishna recovered and a mourning Satyabhama agreed to Naraka's wish.

Even today, Naraka is remembered when people light lamps to dispel the darkness around and in them.

Sita's strength

The Ramayana has many versions, but at the core, it is a poem of love of the ideal man, Rama.

Rama, the avatar of Vishnu, is tasked with the killing of Ravana, the Rakshasa King of Lanka, who troubles the earth with his atrocities.

There are many versions of the Ramayana and most of them tell the story from Rama's perspective.

Sita is the ideal woman, an avatar of the Goddess Laxmi, but her voice is muted or rather muffled in the mainstream, more popular, versions.

Sita in these versions is like the heroine of many Indian movies today, to embellish Rama's image and glory.

These are idealistic versions pandering to a patriarchal society.

But behind every man there was a strong woman, and Sita was a strong woman who supported Ram. Without her, Ram would never win.

Some of the Ramayana versions, written in local languages or the oral traditions, have a different perspective. They show that without a woman, a man is helpless.

One version from Orissa highlights this aspect.

This is my version of the story.

The war between Rama and Ravana had been raging for 12 days and the Lankan Army was on its last legs.

It is the thirteenth day, and finally Ravana and Rama are face to face. This is the last battle of the war.

The battle is fierce, and it tested both to the limits of their strength and skill.

At last, Rama prevails and his arrow strikes Ravana a fatal blow, and the great Ravana falls to the ground.

The earth shakes, and the golden city of Lanka mourns its great king. Sounds of weeping and wailing fill the air. The women of Lanka come out; their hair dishevelled

, their clothes torn, eyes red with weeping.

Sita comes from the Ashoka Vatika and begins comforting and consoling the wailing women.

The wounded are being taken away first and people search for their loved ones.

Broken limbs, severed heads, and gore litter the battleground. The reek of flesh and blood is in the air.

Jackals and vultures are foraging among the dead, and the wailing and laments reach a crescendo.

The light is now fading and there is, at last, an end to the killing and maiming.

Rama, Laxman, Sugreeva, and Hanuman relax at last. They are exhausted and tired.

The survivors also move off slowly as the light fades and twilight falls.

The body of Ravana stirs. There is evil in everyone, but in Ravana, it is a beast much greater than in anyone else.

The evil in Ravana is not dead, it refuses to die. It is a mindless beast, and it forms over the body of Ravana.

The darkness over Ravana takes shape. It is all the evil in the world accumulated by Ravana. It has now come to life.

A fearsome being rises from Ravana's body. It has many heads ravenous for flesh and blood. It has many arms holding fearsome weapons. The heads have eyes that show no soul.

The beast rises and grows. No words come out, but growls and roars. It is everyone's worst nightmare come to life.

Rama and his army are stunned. At the cusp of victory, this calamity has fallen on them.

The beast ravages through the battlefield, killing and drinking the blood of its victims.

An exhausted Rama rushes to do battle with the beast and save his people.

Rama is tired and wounded from the battle and it is with difficulty that he raises his heavy bow and shoots the beast.

Sugreeva, Laxman, and Hanuman join Rama and they battle the beast.

The arrows of Rama do not have any effect on the growling, roaring demon, nor can Laxman stop it.

Sugreeva and Hanuman attack with their maces, but they, too, cannot destroy the beast.

The night is lit up with the funeral pyres of the dead warriors; filled with the sounds of the wounded groaning and crying. The wails of the women add to the misery.

Rama and his friends barely held the demon in check. It takes all their strength just to stop it.

The beast roars, and its glowing eyes add to the fear that everyone feels.

"Lord, we cannot hold it back much longer. My strength is waning," says Sugreeva to Ram.

Even Hanuman is feeling the strain and effort. Laxman says nothing, but there is worry and fear in his eyes.

"What can we do?" asks Rama to Sugreeva. "I have used up all my strength and my arrows now seem to have no effect on the beast."

Dawn is just an hour away when a Jambavan, the old and wise bear of the army, shuffles up.

His black fur streaked with wounds and dripping blood from many wounds, but the old warrior will not give up.

Jambavan's arrival boosts Rama and his friends. They remember his wise counsel, which has saved them from many disasters.

Hopefully, they wait as Jambavan studies the monster straining against the weapons and bonds holding him.

"Lord, I have seen no beast like this. It may be a local manifestation. Let us call Vibhishana," says Jambavan.

Vibhishana, the younger brother of Ravana, is Rama's friend. He arrives, but proves to be clueless and worthless in stopping the beast.

"Lord," says Sugreeva hesitantly, "Mother Sita is wise and has lived among the demons now for some time. She can help us. Please call her."

Rama is reluctant to call his Sita to the gory battlefield. Also, he is the paramount warrior and archer in the world. How can he seek the help of a woman?

But surrounding him are the best warriors in the world, Sugreeva, king of the Vanaras, a formidable warrior who fears no one. Lakshman, the ever-vigilant ferocious warrior who had vanquished even Indrajit. Jambavan, the most experienced warrior of them all. And finally, there was Hanuman, who was destruction personified and who could leap over the ocean, from Rameswaram in India to Lanka.

All of them were helpless in overcoming the beast and dawn was just an hour away.

Rama could feel his strength ebbing. Sugreeva was right, they could not hold for much longer.

Rama looked at his brother and Hanuman and saw in their eyes that they agreed with Sugreeva.

Rama nodded to Vibhishana. "Go to Sita, tell her the problem we face, and seek her help."

It was dawn, and the sun was dispelling the darkness when Sita came into view. Dressed simply and with her customary dignity and calmness, she stood beside Rama and gazed at the demon raging in front of them. Any moment it would break free and be upon them.

Rama looked at his wife standing at his shoulder, fearless and focused. Sita was dressed simply and there were marks from the ordeal she had undergone, but she was still the most beautiful woman he had ever seen. Rama's heart filled with love for his wife and Sita turned and smiled at him as she felt his love in her heart.

"My lord, this is a mindless beast, and your usual weapons will not harm it."

Sita said to Rama, "But I know how to stop it. Give me your bow."

The warriors were surprised, but Rama handed over his heavy bow to Sita.

As the others watched, amazed, the delicate and frail Sita lifted the heavy bow and strung it effortlessly.

"My lord, release the beast. I will distract it and then you can get rid of it," said Sita.

Rama looked with pride at his Sita, as she stood fearlessly with the bow strung and ready to face the beast, which had defeated all of them.

Rama and his friends release the beast. There was a roar of triumph from the demon as it moved towards them.

Sita invoked the five-pointed weapon of Kamadeva, the God of love, from which no one could escape. She placed it on the bow and sent it with an unerring aim to hit the beast on its chest and pierce its heart.

The beast stumbled and slowly sank to its knees. The eyes of the beast no longer looked mindless.

It folded its hand and from it came Ravana's voice.

"Forgive me, mother, release me now, please."

Rama jumped forward, and with one stroke of his sword, he beheaded the monster.

There was silence from the warriors for a moment, and then they raised a great cheer of delight and relief. The Sun had come up and there was light as it dispelled darkness.

The victory was Rama's now. He looked at his wife Sita and said, "my dear, for all our strength and abilities, this victory would not be possible without you."

Sita accepted his words and his love and replied, "My lord, I will always be with you not only during all your victories, but through all your difficulties, trials, or tribulations."

The story also tells us that love is a dominant force against which nothing can prevail.

Without Sita, there would have been no victory for Rama, or rather, without Sita, there is no Rama.

The Power of Forgiveness

There are many stories in our ancient texts that confuse and confound us. They give rise to distress and anger. They repel us when we look at them with current sensibilities.

Those who dislike Hindus also used them to distort the faith.

But these stories are there for a reason. We need to look at them closely and find the lessons we can learn.

There are many stories and beliefs in the various religions around the world which are at odds with current sensibilities.

We should read them and not ignore them because of our cultural sensibilities. That's the way to learn.

One such story is of the Rishi Galava and Princess Madhavi, a disturbing tale at many levels.

This story is often told as the tale of Galava Rishi and his search for the perfect horses to pay his Guru Dakshina. But for me, it is the tale of Madhavi.

Galava was the son and disciple of Rishi Vishwamitra. He was an excellent son and disciple, devoted to his guru.

Vishwamitra felt Galava had learned all he could teach. He blessed him and asked him to set up his own ashram.

Galava asked what was the Guru Dakshina, the teacher's fees, to be paid. Vishwamitra waved him away.

Galava was his son and had worked around the ashram, and Vishwamitra would take no dakshina.

But Galava persisted, and an irritated Vishwamitra told him to get 800 pure white horses with one black ear.

Vishwamitra knew this was an impossible task.

Galava was despondent. Where could he get horses like these? He sought the help of Garuda, who asked him to seek the help of King Yayati.

Yayati was duly met, and the request was made.

Yayati considered himself a great king. But he did not have the horses, nor the money to buy them.

There is all this talk of not refusing a request from a Brahmana... but if Galava was the son of Vishwamitra, he would have been a Kshatriya.

It was Yayati's ego that made him do what he did next. He offered his beautiful daughter Madhavi to Galava Rishi!

"My daughter is the most beautiful woman in the world. I give her to you, trade her for the horses," said Yayati.

"She has a boon; she will give birth to only sons who will all grow up to be great kings and sages. Further, after the birth of each son, she will regain her virginity and become chaste again." Said the proud Yayati.

So, you can see this desire for male offspring is an ancient tradition in our land.

It is horrifying to read that a father did this to his young daughter. But men in their pride destroy daughters even today. In the name of honour and all such nonsense, girls are sacrificed even today in modern India.

Daughters are killed in the womb even today, so then why should we be surprised at Yayati?

The princess was brought forth and handed over. She looked once at her proud father, ignored her docile mother, and stepped forth with Galava.

In those days, they expected a daughter to be obedient to her father. Rama was also obedient to his father, and they praised him for his actions while Madhavi was lost, unheard of. The glass ceiling is nothing new.

The young rishi was focused on his mission and, for him, the beautiful princess was just a travelling companion and a means to his ends.

Galava heard of a king who had the horses he required and he went there. But the king had only 200 horses and Galava was despondent. The King wanted a male heir and the beautiful Madhavi too.

The King proposed a deal. He would keep Madhavi as a wife until she had a son through him. After that, Galava could come and collect her and the 200 horses. They would leave the child behind with the king.

So, it was done. Madhavi stayed a little more than a year. She had a son, Vasumas, who was left behind as she left with the Rishi Galava.

Now Galava knew of two other kings who had the horses he wanted. These kings, too, wanted a male heir.

One look at the beautiful princess and the second king agreed to the same deal. Madhavi to stay till a son was born, then she could go along with the horses with Galava.

So, they bartered the princess three times and Galava collected 600 horses.

Madhavi had three sons, Vasumas, Shibi and Pratardhana, with the three kings.

Galava could not find any more horses as required, but he was not worried. He knew now what he had to do.

He handed over the 600 horses and offered Madhavi as a temporary consort to Vishwamitra. She would live with him till she bore him a son.

Men are men, whether they are kings or sages. Vishwamitra happily accepted.

In due course, she had a son with Vishwamitra, Ashtaka, who later became his father's heir and a great sage.

Galava had paid his Guru Dakshina, he had no further need for Madhavi. She was only a means to an end.

He brought her back to King Yayati. The King decided he had to secure his daughter's future. That meant marriage.

He would marry her off formally, so he arranged for a swyamvar, a gathering of eligible men. The Princess could choose whomsoever she wanted.

On the day of the swyamvar, the princess moved around the gathering of men.

Men eager for an heir, men with lust in their eyes.

The Princess ignored them all and walked to the nearby forest and there she garlanded a tree.

Thus, the beautiful princess chose the forest and became an ascetic meditating on life.

Years passed and Yayati gained heaven and there he became the bosom pal of Indra, the king of gods.

One day, they were sitting and watching the Apsaras dance while sipping soma juice.

That's what men do. All this talk of dance bars being against our culture is just a reflection of colonial hang-ups and Victorian prudishness.

They were discussing who had done the maximum number of yagnas. Yayati's claim that he had done the most angered Indra, who pushed him down from heaven.

Yayati fell to earth and pleaded with Indra to reconsider. Indra agreed that if Yayati could get someone to give him their merits earned through good deeds, Yayati could come back.

Yayati knew he could not ask his sons. He had already once taken his son Puru's youth to indulge his desires.

So, he went in search of his daughter, Madhavi.

The ascetic Madhavi listened to her father, but she could not share her merit, being a woman, with her father.

She called her four sons, the three great kings and the great sage.

As always, sons are their mother's pets and mama's boys. Especially in India.

The sons rushed to their mother and found the decrepit Yayati there. On knowing who he was, they looked at him in anger.

They had not forgotten what had happened to their mother.

But Madhavi was calm. She had found peace in the forest and forgiveness in her heart.

She explained to her sons, forgiveness is a need not for the one you forgive, it is a need for us who forgive.

It clears the mind clouded in anger and soothes the heart. It takes away the pain and directs our thoughts in a better way.

For their mother, the sons forgave Yayati and gave him a quarter of their merit. Yayati thus returned to heaven.

The sons gathered around the mother; they had learnt the power of forgiveness, the most potent but most difficult of all.

The Prince at the Fork

Once, long ago, I travelled to Orissa. This was much before I could afford to travel by flight or even in air-conditioned comfort in trains.

Travel was in three tiers third class and you were happy if you had a confirmed berth so that you could sleep during the night. A top berth was preferable as a lower berth meant someone was always asking you to adjust so that they could share your berth.

There was no point in protesting as these were local travellers traveling within a section of the route. They felt it was their right to do so, and protesting could lead to trouble for you from other locals. The railway employees would strategically stay away.

The middle berth would be uncomfortable.

I had a top berth and was happy, but the night was cold and I had no blankets. I was shivering when the old man in the lower berth saw me. He quietly took out a blanket from his bag and offered it to me. This started another transient train friendship.

He was an old man from Calcutta and we started talking; I was a young man of 28 and he was over 70 years old, a spry wise man who had been a teacher. He kept me regaled with many stories. One story which he told me from the Ramayana I had never heard before and have not heard it since. But it is lovely and stuck in my mind. Here is my retelling. I hope you like it.

Vishwamitra the rishi wanted to conduct a yagna in the forest. The forest had many rakshasas who would try to disrupt it.

So Vishwamitra wanted to get a royal prince who would protect the yagna. Vishwamitra himself could have ensured the protection of the yagna, but his purpose was to identify a prince who was suitable to be groomed into a great King.

Vishwamitra knew the use of divine weapons, which were not known to many people. As a former king, he also knew the duties of a ruler. He wanted to impart this to a suitable prince.

He had heard the people praising the princes of Ayodhya and went to Dashrath, the King of Ayodhya.

The King was reluctant to send his sons into so perilous a venture, but was afraid that Vishwamitra might curse him and his kingdom.

"I will send my second son Bharata and the younger one, Shatrughan, with you. I cannot send my eldest son Rama, as he is the crown prince." Said Dashrath.

Vishwamitra agreed, and with the two princes accompanying him, proceeded on their journey.

A short time later, they came to a fork in the road. Vishwamitra stopped and told the princes.

"One road is short and direct to the place we want to go. The other is longer, more fearsome, and swarms with Rakshasas. Which should we take?"

The two princes immediately said let us take the shorter safer route. Vishwamitra silently turned and took the princes back to Ayodhya.

"These boys are not suitable, so send the other two with me demanded Vishwamitra.

The king must protect yagnas and rishis. Dashrath had no choice.

But he was reluctant to send his favourite son Rama into danger. He proposed to go with Vishwamitra himself with his army. But Vishwamitra refused. He wanted the two princes alone.

Dashrath was in agony. He feared to send his Rama into the dangers of the forest but also feared the wrath of Vishwamitra.

His guru Vasishta chided Dashrath. "Vishwamitra is a great rishi. He has both spiritual powers and knowledge of arms. If he insists on taking the princes, it is for a greater purpose. It will benefit the princes too. Let them go."

So, Rama and Lakshmana started on the journey and were excited to know they would have to fight the rakshasas to protect the yagna. They had not been in an actual fight, not seen rakshasas till then.

They wanted to learn everything Vishwamitra could tell them. The rishi advised them to be patient.

They soon arrived at the fork in the road. The Rishi told them what he had told Bharata and Shatrughan. One fork was easy and direct, the other fearsome, long, and filled with rakshasas.

Rama immediately chose the longer, more difficult road, and Lakshmana agreed. Vishwamitra asked why did Rama choose the more difficult path.

"We are going with you to protect the yagna from rakshasas. We need to learn about them before we meet them in force. This road will give us that knowledge. If you want to get knowledge, you must be prepared to face difficulties and work hard and long."

Vishwamitra was happy he had found the prince he wanted, someone whom he could train to be a proper King.

You hold the answers in your hand

Indian folk tales can be simple, most folk tales are. But the message they convey can be complex and thought-provoking.

I heard this story in Madhya Pradesh a long time ago. A simple story, but a story that tells us that most often the answer to our question can be found within us.

In a small village in Mandsaur, there lived an old lady. She had no name. Everyone called her Ma, which means mother.

She lived alone, a gentle, wise old woman, and the villagers often came to her for help and advice.

They came and asked her when it would rain, when to plant the seeds, how to cure a fever, how to bring an errant husband back, and so many other such issues.

She listened to their problems; she listened well and gave her advice in simple terms.

She never judged, and often the villagers went to her just so that they could talk and lighten their problems.

There was an ambitious young man from the village, Veer Singh. He had gone away to the capital city and spent a year there.

After coming back from there, he preened himself and put on airs. He had seen the king himself once!

He kept putting himself forward and offering advice, but was often ignored in the village councils. But the village panchayat would often consult the old lady and always follow her advice.

Veer Singh was upset and vowed to show the village that the old woman was a fake. He spent his days thinking about how to get the better of the old woman. He neglected his fields; he neglected his family while he spent sleepless nights thinking about how to show up the old woman.

One day he caught a small bird, a theethar, an Indian Partridge common in this area.

He kept his hand behind his back; the bird hidden between his hands.

He stood before the old lady where she sat pounding grain in her pestle. There were other people around.

"Oh Ma," he said, "everyone says you are the wisest person here and know everything. Can you tell me what I hold in my hands?"

The old lady looked at Veer Singh and smiled and spoke

"Son, I never said I am the wisest person in the village, and there are many things I don't know. But what you hold in your hands is a small bird."

She had heard the faint flutter of wings of the trapped bird.

Veer Singh was surprised, but he thought quickly. "Oh Ma, you are right. It is a bird, but tell me whether it is alive or dead," he asked triumphantly.

If the old woman said the bird was alive, Veer Singh decided he would crush the bird inside his hands and show the dead bird. If she said it was a dead bird, he would release it and all would see it fly and know the old lady was mistaken.

The Old lady, wise in the ways of men, smiled at him gently. "Son," she said, "your answer is in your hands. Seek it within you".

Veer Singh was intelligent. He realised the old woman had indeed given the perfect answer. He brought his hands forward and gently released the bird. The bird flew away and Veer Singh's jealousy went with it.

He realised that if he believed in himself and worked hard, he would never have to be jealous of anyone. The answer to his search for success was within himself, not in bringing someone down.

A lesson we all need to learn and let the bird of jealousy to fly away from us.

Notes and suggested readings

Ancient Indian writing is a vast treasure house of stories. The biggest sources are the two epics, the Ramayana and the Mahabharata.

The Mahabharata and the Ramayana are known all over India and a basic knowledge of the story is known to most Indians irrespective of the religion they follow.

For those who have not read the Mahabharata or the Ramayana, I suggest the following books as initial reading. They are mainstream versions and may not contain the stories that I have retold here.

1. Amar Chitra Katha Comics has an enormous collection of such stories. They also have comics with an abridged version of both epics.
2. The Ramayana by C. Rajagopalachari, published by Bharatiya Vidya Bhavan, remains a classic. It is written in simple language and is a concise version of the epics.
3. The Ramayana by Kamala Subramaniam, also published by Bharatiya Vidya Bhavan, is a more detailed version, but still only an abridged version of the original epic.
4. The Mahabharata by C. Rajagopalachari, published by Bharatiya Vidya Bhavan, remains a classic. It is written in simple language and is a concise version of the Epic and yet captures its essence.
5. The Mahabharata by Kamala Subramaniam, also published by Bharatiya Vidya Bhavan, is a more detailed version in a single volume.
6. For those interested in exploring folklore, the works of A. K

      Ramanujan will be of interest.

7. Irawati Karve's "Yugantar" is a lovely book exploring the characters of the Mahabharata.

There are many, many more, but the above should give you an excellent base.

There are many other versions and modern writers have explored the epics, giving their own viewpoint and creating fresh stories.

I have read and heard many versions of the stories in the Ramayana and the Mahabharata.

During my travels and posting in different parts of India, I found that each area had local stories and songs about the characters in the two Epics.

This sparked of my lifelong love and search for stories based in the epics but with a local twist.

The stories included in this volume are only a few of those stories being told and retold by the people of India over the centuries.

I hope you enjoy reading them.

I would love to hear from you at my email id krishnanrr2622@gmail.com.

My Facebook page is R. Radhakrishnan

Did you love *The Book of Ancient Wisdom*? Then you should read *Indian Mythology*[1] by R RADHAKRISHNAN!

The Rishis, the wise men of ancient India, were in a dilemma. They had compiled the Vedas, the rules of behaviour, and Dharma had been conceptualised or framed.

Dharma, you could consider as a mission statement for life.

But how to reach it to the people so they could understand? How to ensure that people listened to the lessons? One of those wise men then came up with the brilliant idea of telling stories which would interest people and also have the required knowledge to learn from.

So were born the marvellous stories or epics of Hinduism. The stories have in them ideals, morals, rules of life and so much more. It brilliantly packaged these ideals in stories that enchant and yet teach.

---

1. https://books2read.com/u/mqE17Q

2. https://books2read.com/u/mqE17Q

This small book has some of those stories of ancient wisdom. R.Radhakrishnan retells and interprets those tales simply and links them to our everyday life. These are tales that gently guide even as they amuse you with thier wit and imagination.

Read more at https://sites.google.com/view/rradhakrishnan.

Also by R RADHAKRISHNAN

The Temples of India
The Temples of India: Somnathapura, Mysore

Travellers Tales
Rustic Romeo

Standalone
The Colors of Life
The Temples of India : Guruvayur
Indian Mythology
The Book of Ancient Wisdom

Watch for more at https://sites.google.com/view/rradhakrishnan.

About the Author

Radhakrishnan is a traveller, storyteller and a seeker of stories. In a corporate career of four decades, he travelled all over India listening and accumulating stories.

He loves to explore the similarities in the many versions found in the different regions of India and the lessons they teach even as they entertain. This book brings alive these stories from the folktales, epics and the songs that Indians have been telling or singing over the centuries. They bring to life an ageless, ancient and yet timeless India.

Radhakrishnan now lives in the beautiful city of Cochin in the state of Kerala with his family.